DON'T TAKE YOUR

DREAMS

TO THE GRAVE

JIMMIE BRATCHER

Contents

Introduction

I assume that you hold this book in your hands because, like me, you have that gnawing in your heart that just won't go away...a dream. Well, may I be the first to say congratulations because you're taking steps in the right direction—steps that may really turn your life upside-down or right-side-up. You'll never know till you try.

Dreams are what make our lives exciting. Dreams can be mysterious...many times divine pieces of information that can reveal our true self, our destinies. I hope every day your life is full of dreams. I hope you have a dream for you future, for your marriage, for your kids, and for every area of your life. I hope when it's time to pass from this world to the next you can look back at your life and see dreams fulfilled. My goal is to never quit dreaming; no matter how old I get or how impossible it seems, I think we should just "go for it" and live our dreams.

With everything great there are great costs and great risks. You have to be prepared to face and live with the risks to live your dreams. For me, I got to the point where the pain of not living my dreams was so great that I was willing to lay down all I had accomplished just to live my life directed by the dreams in my heart. Now, here is my disclaimer: Don't go quit your job and wreck your life and then email me about how it didn't work. Be wise about the risks, talk to your spouse, talk to people you trust, and most of all talk to God and listen to your heart.

Here's a quote that some attribute to Mark Twain: "Twenty years from now you will be more disappointed by the things that you didn't do than by the ones you did do." Maybe you're like I was, in a place of transition. Maybe you're nearing retirement or maybe it's just time for you to make a change. At any rate, *Don't Take Your Dreams to the Grave* without at least giving them your best shot.

My total goal in writing this book is to encourage you. In the pages of this book you will find years of my pain and years of my victory. I share them with you in the hope that they may help you avoid some of the mistakes I made. I hope that while reading this book you will find the real you and not be afraid to show the real you to the world.

Peace,

Jimmie

CHAPTER ONE

Don't Take Your Dream to the Grave

Have you ever felt that the person you show to the outside world is not the person you really are? That inside you is a person you like better than the person other people see? Do you ever feel that this inside person—the real you—is screaming to get out but can't? Do you fear that the dream you once had for your life is passing beyond reach and that it is too late to become the person you always wanted to be or to do with your life what you've always wanted to do?

If you answered yes to any of these questions, don't be discouraged; you are not alone. Many other

1

people are in the same boat. I know, I know, I hear you: "Well, *that* makes me feel a *whole* lot better!" I just want you to understand that you are not the first or the only person who has felt this way. Even more, I want you to know that there is hope. As long as you are alive and breathing, it's never too late to release

Do you fear that the dream you once had for your life is passing beyond reach?

the real you. It's never too late to pursue your life's dream. I know because I used to feel the same way you do...until the day I resolved not to take my dream to the grave!

One morning, at the age of 45, I woke up wondering just who I had become, and to be brutally honest, I didn't like myself at all. Over the years my values and life vision had been clouded and replaced by other things, and I hated it. Don't get me wrong; they were all good things, but they were things that required me to be someone I was not. Sure, I was a born-again follower of Jesus Christ and happily married with the two best kids in the world. I was even in full-time ministry as an associate pastor of a very successful church. But every time I looked in the mirror I asked, "Who is this man?" It wasn't that I had a bad life—I didn't. I simply had become unhappy with the life I was living because it did not really reflect who I was on the inside.

For years I had been burying my dream, making my life conform to the way others thought it should be. Facing the issue of the man I had become was one of the most intense and challenging things I have ever done. As I examined my life I realized first of all that I was responsible for making myself the way I was. No one forced me to hide my true self. I had made a choice, which meant that I also could choose to unmake this false person I was showing to the world and rebuild my life according to who I really was. I had all the necessary tools. So bit by bit, piece by piece, little by little, I started undoing what had taken me and my "religious" mind-set years to build. It wasn't easy or simple, but in the end it was worth every bit of the effort it took. Releasing the real me to follow my life's dream was the best thing that ever happened to me (except for finding Jesus) because it put me in touch with what God had wanted for my life all along.

I started to release the man I had been hiding for years and turn him loose in my world. Today, I am happier, healthier, and more satisfied than at any other time in my life. I have found more peace, truth, and fulfillment in life because I am learning to allow the Holy Spirit to work and reveal Jesus through my personality without apology or regret. I will not take my dream to the grave.

You don't have to either if you are willing to go on a personal journey of self-discovery. Let me encourage you to pursue your dream and press forward to become the person God meant for you to be. That's what this book is all about. Although it probably won't answer all your questions, my prayer is that it will help get you started on your way. Your journey may be rough or scary at first, but hang on tight and I promise that, in the end, you will be glad you took it.

Nothing is more exciting or fulfilling than unlocking the "real you"—the true person you are inside—and letting that person live the life God has always intended for you to live. Does that sound like a dream come true? It is. After all, dream fulfillment is what we're talking about. Don't take your dream to the grave. Start today to learn how to reclaim the real person locked inside you, to break out of your self-made prison, and to pursue the dream God has placed in your heart and wants to bring to reality through you. It doesn't matter how old you are or what has happened in your past. What matters is reconnecting with that God-given dream inside you, reaching forward to claim it and allowing God to bring it to pass in your life. No matter where you are, God will start right there and take you where He has always wanted you to go.

A Dream Come True

I will always remember July 25, 2002. I had been in Macon, Georgia, for ten days recording my second CD, *Something Better*. It was my second trip to Macon working on the project. Macon is a city rich with music history and I loved recording there. Now I was on my way to meet my wife, Sherri, in Jackson, Mississippi. I was scheduled to minister there that weekend, and Sherri was flying in to meet me.

On the way, I couldn't restrain my excitement about the work that the band and I had just completed. This was the first time that I had a horn section on any of my music and man, did it sound fantastic! I was so excited that I called my bassist, Jeff Wollenberg, and played the songs to him over my cell phone!

I had known Jeff only a few months but he had quickly become one of my best friends. We spoke several times a day on the phone. Jeff had played on *Something Better* and even helped write one of my most requested songs on that CD, "Get Out The Boat."

Jeff came from a pretty shattered past. He had been a meth dealer and spent four years in federal prison for his crime. Two years into his term, Jeff believed on Jesus and his life was transformed. He spent the rest of his time, in his words, "in Bible school behind the wall." When Jeff entered prison he was a wired-to-the-wall meth freak; when he got out he was a wired-to-the-wall *Jesus* freak. One of the first things Jeff did after he got out was to go right back to the clubs where he had played before prison; only now things were different. Jeff was different and all his friends knew it.

When Jeff left prison he had a dream of rebuilding his life and his family and of some day returning to prison, not as an inmate of the federal court system, but as an ambassador of Jesus. All of Jeff's dreams came true. He remarried and reconciled with his children. Then came the day in April 2002 when I invited Jeff to go into some prisons with me and share what Jesus had done for him. For Jeff, it was truly a dream come true. I was the instrument for the fulfillment of a desire God had planted deep in Jeff's heart. Jeff was the happiest man on earth that week as, day after day, we went to different prisons playing music and sharing our faith. I remembered it like it was yesterday.

Now, three months later, it was July 25, 2002, and Sherri and I were in Jackson, Mississippi. Late that night my cell phone rang. I hate phone calls in the middle of the night; they are almost always bad news. Such was the case with this call. A man was sobbing uncontrollably on the other end of the line, and it took me a while to figure out who it was.

It was Jeff's pastor.

"Jimmie," he said between sobs, "Jeff has passed away."

I was stunned. The news knocked the breath right out of me. Jeff dead? How could it be? I could hardly believe that this man, my friend, had passed from this life to the next just like that. But it was true.

Jeff had been lying in bed with his wife reading his Bible. Finding something in the Word that spoke to him, he reached for a marker to highlight the passage, let out a wheeze...and went to Heaven. That was it. He was gone.

I hated that day...everything about it. Jeff is a great man and I miss him very much. There is much about Jeff's death that I don't understand, but I find great consolation in at least two things. First, I know that today Jeff is in Heaven with the Savior he loved so much. Second, I know that Jeff didn't take his dreams to the grave.

Jeff believed that he would be happy again and he was. His wife and kids loved him and everybody knew it. He lived to see the dreams he had for his family come to pass. He touched his friends with the same love with which Jesus had touched him. More than 1300 of them came to his visitation. It was a remarkable sight.

He lived to see the dreams he had for his family come to pass.

Jeff dreamed of playing music that glorified God, and we did that. He dreamed of going back to prison, taking with him the message of Christ that had changed his life. That, too, came to pass. When the time came for Jeff to pass from earth to Heaven he had left no dreams unfulfilled. Sure, I know there were things that Jeff wanted and expected to do, but his brief life in Christ on this earth was spent in white-hot pursuit of the dreams His Lord had planted in his heart.

Some people might shake their heads at Jeff's story and say, "How sad! Someone so young and full of promise to die so unexpectedly. What a waste."

I couldn't disagree more. Sure, I still miss Jeff—I miss him a lot. But his life wasn't wasted. He may not have had many years as a disciple of Jesus before he went home, but the years he did have were lived to the fullest for his Lord. God does not measure the character of our lives by length of days but by faithfulness of heart, and by that standard, Jeff measured up.

Whether short or long, a life spent pursuing one's God-given dreams is never wasted and a life lived full-throttle for Christ is never in vain. It's never too late to start pursuing your dream. No matter what your circumstances, don't let regrets of the past keep you from moving ahead to your future. In Jesus your best days are still ahead.

PERSONAL DREAM JOURNAL

＊

_____

_____

_____

_____

_____

_____

_____

_____

_____

_____

_____

_____

_____

_____

_____

_____

_____

_____

_____

_____

_____

_____

_____

_____

CHAPTER TWO

The Invasion

Jeff and I are alike in some ways, at least where our early lives are concerned. We were both druggies and we both had family problems caused by drugs. We both found Jesus, and here is where it gets a little weird. Jeff's coming to Jesus released him to pursue his dreams. When I got saved, I ended up in a situation that resulted in my suppressing my dreams for years, almost to the point where they disappeared altogether.

In 1976 I was a 22-year-old, drug-taking, hard-drinking divorcé with a three-year-old son named Jason, over whom I shared joint custody with my then ex-wife, Sherri. Don't be confused This is the same Sherri who is my wife today. After we got our lives straight in Jesus, we remarried. As a matter of fact, I got saved the *very same day* Sherri and I remarried.

Ever since I was a kid I had dreamed of being a rock star. When I was 16 I dropped out of school to follow that dream. For six years I had tried my best to live the rock and roll lifestyle, along with everything that went with it.

> *Ever since I was a kid I had dreamed of being a rock star.*

Sherri and I first met at a Black Sabbath concert. Both of us were high on LSD. We got together, abused barbiturates together, and before long Sherri was pregnant. We got married—a union we now refer to as "the marriage made in hell." It was a drug-soaked highly abusive relationship that lasted three years. Things got so bad that my grandmother, Granny, paid for our divorce. You *know* that your marriage is messed up when Granny pays for the divorce!

We did get divorced but over time started seeing each other again. Joint custody of Jason played a big part in that, but our love for each other was there also; we just didn't know what to do with it. Sometime during that period, Sherri made a commitment to Christ while watching *The 700 Club* and began attending (with Jason) a small church in the country. God also was working on me, although I didn't know it at the time. At church Jason went forward and requested prayer for his daddy to come home. Months later Sherri and I decided to get married again. We couldn't live with each other, but it seemed also that we couldn't live without each other!

We got a marriage license and took it to the pastor of the church where Sherri and Jason were attending. We handed the marriage license to the pastor and said, "We want to get married tonight." He looked at us and replied, "I'm not going to join this mess together." Later he changed his mind and said, looking at me, "I will marry you tonight on one condition: that you promise to accept Jesus as your Savior." I said, "Sure." In my mind I was thinking, *"Talk's cheap and I don't mind lying."*

Then the pastor said, "You're going to accept Christ tonight. Are you ready?"

"I'm here," I replied. I thought I was being cool but God saw it as faith. In my wildest dreams I never expected God to show up, but I walked out of that room a new man. God invaded my life when I wasn't looking, and my life was radically transformed through a personal relationship with Jesus Christ by faith. In addition, Sherri and I both walked out that night completely addiction-free.

Trapped by Religion

Although my life was transformed through my relationship with Jesus I soon realized that *Like many other Christians both before and after me, I got caught in the confusion between relationship and religion.* not everything that calls itself Christian is an exact representation of the person of Jesus Christ. Like many other Christians both before and after me, I got caught in the confusion between relationship and religion. Religion is the enemy of relationship. Relationship is what we enter into when we give our hearts to Jesus in faith with repentance of our sins. Religion is the dry, empty prison of man-made rules and regulations that masquerades as relationship. A relationship with Jesus frees us to become the people we were meant to be, fulfilled and fruitful. Religion locks us into the straitjacket of others' expectations.

Jeff Wollenberg came to Jesus and was liberated to pursue his dreams. Jesus liberated me, too, but I allowed myself to be deceived by the desire to seek the approval of others. As a result, I spent many years trapped by religion, doing religious works involving self-sacrifice and focusing on outward appearance. The whole time I thought I was pleasing God when, in fact, I was only hurting myself and the people I loved the most. I allowed my dreams to become clouded and replaced by other things. Those other things were others' dreams. They were good dreams and well-meaning dreams, but they were not my dreams.

I blame no one but myself for what happened all those years. No one held me hostage. No one forced me to suppress my dreams in exchange for the dull ritual of religion. I did it of my own free will. This does not mean that the tools of control and manipulation were never used on me; they were. But still, it was my decision to give in to those tools. It was my decision to lay down my dreams for my destiny and to take up something else. I had allowed my dreams to be stolen under the banner of religious performance.

Slowly I discovered that the man God made me to be was eroding away like a rain-soaked hillside. Piece by piece my personality was slipping away. I'm not talking about the destructive behaviors of my past or my old sinful ways; I am talking about my *personality*—the "real me" deep inside, the person God originally made me to be. The more I looked, the more I realized that the "real me" was a "wild man" bound in the shackles of religion and screaming to be let loose.

Watch Out for the Wild Man

Like me, you have a "wild man" deep inside you, too. Everybody does. I'm talking about the wild man who was ready to risk it all for one good time; the one who would party till dawn, spend an entire week's pay in a weekend, and wake up on Sunday morning broke and with a headache and call it a good time. I'm talking about the wild man who is willing to risk everything, to go out on a limb to chase a dream that everyone else calls foolish.

What happened to that person?

"Well," you might say, "I got saved and sanctified and cleansed by the blood of Jesus." Okay. So did I. So what? Did salvation and sanctification kill your wild personality? Is the blood of Jesus toxic to the wild man? Once we're saved, are we supposed to become mild-mannered wimps like Clark Kent or are we simply suppressing the Superman God intended us to be? Have we hidden our wild side under the thin veneer of religious performance?

16

I don't know about you, but one day I just got tired of hiding, tired of living incognito. One day my real personality broke through again, and I am so glad it did!

Don't misunderstand me. When I talk about being wild I am not advocating backsliding and going back to our old sinful ways. Why would anyone want to do that? There is nothing in that direction except death and destruction. I'm also not promoting some kind of elitist's hyperspiritual craziness that is out of touch with reality and in no way relates to our culture. Releasing the wild man inside doesn't mean going off the deep end.

What I am advocating is reconnecting with the wild man inside of you.

What I am advocating is reconnecting with the wild man inside of you, lining him up with the Word of God, and releasing him on the unsuspecting world of your life. Just think what you could do if you took all that wild energy bottled up inside and focused it on good things, godly things, constructive things. Instead, folks like you and me come to Jesus and somehow lose all of our fire. We sit back and watch as our sharp edge is ground dull by religion. And all the while we're unaware that what we are really doing is allowing outside forces to conform us to an image other than Jesus.

Don't Take Your Dreams to the Grave

Our goal in life as believers is to become like Jesus. Romans 8:29 says that God predestined us "to be conformed to the image of His Son." Jesus is a wild Savior. Everywhere He went people said of Him, "We have never seen anything like this before." Jesus did unbelievable things, not just in the miracles He performed, but also in the way He communicated with people. He offended and scandalized the religious people of His day by readily defying social customs and behavior patterns when they stood in the way of His reaching out to people who needed Him.

Jesus is unique. Never before or since has there been anyone on earth like Him, and there won't be again until He returns. Nevertheless, our calling as Christians is to seek to become like Jesus. Following His example, we can be transformed into His image. Nothing will bring greater satisfaction to our lives than to allow the Holy Spirit to form the likeness of Jesus in us. Being like Jesus means being radical and wild because that's the way He was.

Wildness is not primarily a matter of physical appearance or outward manifestations, even though that is what most people would look for. The wildness I'm talking about is a wildness of the heart, and the heart is where God looks. First Samuel 16:7b says, "For the Lord does not see as man sees; for man looks at the outward appearance, but the Lord looks at the heart." When God looks at our heart, He wants to see the image of His Son. That's where our focus needs to be, not on outward manifestations or in conforming to others' expectations.

Wild people don't conform; they break the mold. They follow their own dreams because that is what makes them come alive. Sometimes people spend years helping others pursue their dreams, and this too is an honorable pursuit. There is nothing wrong with working for someone else's dream. The problem arises when people allow themselves to become deadened to their own dreams in the process and end up taking their dreams to the grave. The world needs to see what will happen when a few wild people follow their dreams. In *Wild at Heart*, author John Eldredge tells of browsing in a bookstore one day when he came across a statement by a man named Gil Bailie that changed his life forever. That statement captures the essence of what I mean when I say we need to release the wild man inside us:

Don't ask yourself what the world needs. Ask yourself what makes you come alive, and go do that, because what the world needs is people who have come alive.[1]

---

1. Gil Bailie, quoted in John Eldredge, *Wild at Heart* (Nashville: Thomas Nelson Publishers, 2001), 200.

Don't Take Your Dreams to the Grave

What makes *you* come alive? What gets *your* fire burning? Answer that and you will reconnect with your dream. Your dream is directly related to the wild personality inside you. Connect with your dream and pursue it, and people will see you coming down the street and say, "Watch out for the wild man!"

Wild Donkey or Fruitful Bough?

All of us have defining moments in life: events or discoveries that define who we really are. Those are the moments when the whole world seems to stop and something divine is instilled in our hearts and etched in our memories. We can neither create nor predict defining moments; they come unexpectedly and unbidden. Many times we don't even realize a defining moment occurred until days, months, or even years later. Certainly, coming to Jesus and being saved is a defining moment. Another defining moment may be the day we decided, consciously or unconsciously, to

What makes you come alive? What gets your fire burning? Answer that and you will reconnect with your dream.

subordinate our dreams to follow the dictates of religion. For me, a defining moment came the day I decided to break out of that religious trap and become the man God created me to be.

Chapter 49 of the Book of Genesis describes a defining moment in the lives of Jacob's 12 sons. Jacob, old and near death, has gathered his sons around his bed and is speaking his final words to them. Addressing each of his sons in turn, he speaks of their past and present and prophesies to them concerning their future. I want to zero in on one verse in particular, verse 22, where Jacob speaks of Joseph, his most beloved son. Joseph, of course, is the son who was sold into slavery by his jealous brothers and who later rose to become the prime minister of Egypt. Of this most illustrious son Jacob says:

Joseph is a fruitful bough, a fruitful bough by a well; his branches run over the wall (Genesis 49:22).

A "fruitful bough"? I don't know about you but this description of Joseph struck me as really lame. What the heck is a "fruitful bough"? That phrase doesn't even begin to capture anything of Joseph's character or personality. It seemed a strange description, so I did a little digging and discovered something very interesting. Consider the same verse as rendered in *The Message*:

> *Joseph is a wild donkey, a wild donkey by a spring, spirited donkeys on a hill* (Genesis 49:22, The Message).

A wild donkey! Now that's more like it! For me, "wild donkey" captures more of the spirit of who Joseph was.

Think about it: Joseph, a teenage dreamer, slave, prison inmate, and dream interpreter who rose from slavery to prime minister in one day and rescued not only his family but also the entire nation of Egypt from famine. It takes a wild man to do things like that.

The different translations of this verse provide a perfect example of what religion can do to our personality: It can take a wild donkey, with all its spirit, brashness, independence, and unpredictability and turn it into a fruitful bough that is safe, innocuous, and tame. If the original translators of the King James Version of the Bible had gone with the donkey imagery in this verse, they most likely would have used the word *"ass"* as in jackass, and the verse would probably have read: "Joseph is a wild ass." Now *that* would have *really* turned Joseph loose as the wild man he really was!

So, then, what are you—a wild donkey or a fruitful bough? Too many times as Christians we relate our wild nature only to our past sinful life. Although that is an accurate picture as far as it goes, it doesn't go far enough. The picture is incomplete. When we came to Christ, two major defining moments occurred. First, we were "crucified with Christ" as Paul says in Galatians 2:20 and, second, we became "new creatures" in Christ according to 2 Corinthians 5:17. I believe that if we regard our wild-natured personality as something that was nailed to the cross with Jesus or left behind as part of the "old life" that has passed away, we will miss out on a huge part of the life God wants us to live.

God created each of us with unique personalities and characteristics and He enjoys us just as we are. If your nature is to be wild, then you need to be wild even if religion wants to tame you. I am sick and tired of seeing believers portrayed by the world as powerless wimps, out of touch, bland, and generic. Those are not the kind of believers I hang around with. Nor does it describe the tens of thousands of believers I minister to every year. Most of the Christians I meet are in touch, relevant, strong, and ready to make an impact on their world.

Who are you and what defines your life? Are you a wild donkey or a tame Christian pussycat? Who shapes the image of who you should be? Do you get your image from Jesus or do you allow others to shape you according to their picture? As long as you allow your life to be shaped and directed by other people—no matter how well-meaning they might be—you will never realize your true self or fulfill your God-given destiny. There will always be somebody ready to tell you how you are supposed to dress or how you are supposed to wear your hair or what kind of car you should drive or how you should "act." If you allow yourself to get caught in that mode of trying to please men, your life will become like mine was for so many years: nothing but a big fat religious performance far from the abundant life Jesus came to give. Instead of being true to yourself and your God-given dreams and destiny, you will simply be up on a stage performing for a crowd whose tastes can change as quickly as the weather. Take it from me, that kind of life is a fast train to burnout and disillusionment. Don't get on that track.

No Pretense

During His ministry on earth Jesus embraced all kinds of people: the rich and the poor, the sick and the healthy, the outcasts and the influential.

Never did He ask any of them for a performance, but He always regarded them with tenderness and compassion. In fact, the only people He ever really came down hard on were the Pharisees and other Jewish religious leaders of the day. More than once Jesus called them hypocrites. The word comes from the world of Greek theatre and refers to an actor under an assumed character, a stage player who used a series of masks onstage to disguise his true identity. Jesus called the Pharisees hypocrites because they were not who they pretended to be. They were play-acting, hiding their true prideful, sinful selves under a polished mask of religious piety and respectability.

All of us have different masks that we put on, depending on who is around, and the place we wear them the most is at church.

If Jesus was displeased with the Pharisees who pretended to be something they were not, why wouldn't He be displeased with us when we do the same thing? All of us have different masks that we put on, depending on who is around, and the place we wear them the most is at church.

Don't Take Your Dreams to the Grave

Which one of us in our church-going experience has never encountered "The Zone," that magical region somewhere between the parking lot and the front door of the church building in which an amazing transformation takes place? You're in the car with your wife (or husband) and the kids. It's Sunday and the morning has not gone well at home. The kids were cranky and slow to get moving, and then they didn't want to eat their breakfast. You and your spouse were fussing and fighting all the way to church, and as you pull into the parking lot you have one hand on the steering wheel while the other is occupied with a "Big Daddy Smackdown" on the kids in the backseat who are still cranky. You park the car, gather yourselves together as much as is possible, and walk toward the building. That's when you enter "The Zone."

Something amazing happens in "The Zone." By the time you get to the door you are cool, calm, and collected, big Bible under your arm, ear-to-ear smile plastered on your face, nodding pleasantly at everyone you see: "Good morning! How ya' doin'? Praise the Lord! Ain't God great!"

Give me a break!

Why do we feel we have to be somebody other than ourselves? I believe it is due to the pressure we feel to conform to religious expectations rather than to the image of Christ. Our church culture has certain expectations that we must live up to if we are going to be accepted. So we give it our best, put on our best mask and try to cover up the flaws and faults that we all have and pretend that we are all right when really we are not. Deep inside we want so badly to show people who we really are, but we are afraid that they will not like the "real me" and reject us. So we continue to play the game. We continue to hide our true self from others until eventually we begin to lose sight of who we really are. Some people get so caught up playing a role that they never find themselves again.

One of the saddest commentaries on modern church life is that we hide our true selves from each other because we feel we cannot trust each other to love and accept each other as we are. What a tragedy: *God's house is not a safe place!* Rather than a refuge where we can find healing, deliverance, and wholeness, God's house has become a place where masks are the fashion of the day and we use them to hide our brokenness, loneliness, fear, and other dysfunctions from public view. I don't know about you but I am ready to take all my masks and burn them once and for all.

God's Safe House

I was in the Midwest holding an evangelistic event in a church of several hundred. During one of the morning services a man in his mid-20s responded to receive Jesus. That evening I arrived at the service early and was hanging out in the sanctuary when I saw this same young man. I walked over to him and said, "You made the right decision this morning to receive Jesus."

"Oh, I was already a Christian," he replied. "I have just been backslidden for the last several years. I have been struggling with a drug problem and haven't been coming to church because I was afraid of what all the people would think of me."

I grabbed him by the shoulders and said, "Listen to me! This is God's house and you are always welcome here. Whether you're straight or stoned, you come to God's house every time the door is open and let God minister to you and it won't be long before you won't need or want to take drugs anymore."

It's a sad thing to know that it's not safe to have a problem in church. It's even sadder to realize that many people stay away from the house of God out of fear of what other people will think of them. We should just make up our minds that we are not going to allow other people to come between Jesus and us and that we are going to make a commitment to be in His house. That commitment may be the first step in dropping our masks and reclaiming our true self, the "wild man" deep inside.

In *The 7 Habits of Highly Successful People,* author Stephen Covey talks about having a personal constitution. I think many Christians need just such a thing. Covey says that a personal constitution is a set of laws that are extremely difficult to alter and he compares it to the Constitution of the United States. We need to have as part of our personal constitution that we will go to God's house regardless of what anybody thinks and that we will go to God's house unmasked, just as we are, "warts and all," not trying to hide our problems or our weaknesses.

For most of us who are so well trained in role playing, going unmasked is a pretty scary proposition. Nevertheless, we owe it to ourselves, our families, our church, and the world to learn to allow the real person we are to come out unashamed. Think of what a relief it will be to no longer have to hide who we really are or what we're really going through!

I have discovered that I am at my happiest when I am around people with whom I can be myself, people with whom I don't have to pretend and who accept me as I am. Those are the people I love to hang out with because they don't expect me to "perform" or to be somebody I'm not.

It's time to drop the masks and set aside the confining entrapments of religion.

What does it mean to reclaim and release the "wild man" inside us? It means learning to be ourselves. It means learning to live our lives the way God intended. He expects nothing else of us and we should expect nothing else of each other.

It's time to drop the masks and set aside the confining entrapments of religion. It's time to reclaim the joy and intimacy of relationship with the Lord that we had when we were first saved. It's time to rediscover the dream we were meant to fulfill. There is a wild man inside each of us and it's time to let him loose!

PERSONAL DREAM JOURNAL

_____

_____

_____

_____

_____

_____

_____

_____

_____

_____

_____

_____

_____

_____

_____

_____

_____

_____

_____

_____

_____

_____

_____

31

_____
_____
_____
_____
_____
_____
_____
_____
_____
_____
_____
_____
_____
_____
_____
_____
_____
_____
_____
_____
_____
_____

CHAPTER THREE

Don't Let Your Dreams Die

As I said in the last chapter, from a young age I dreamed of being a rock star. I did whatever I could as a kid to follow that dream and, by the time I was in my mid-teens, I was a decent guitarist. Of course, in my mind, the "rock scene" was not just the music and the tours but also the drugs and the alcohol and the women, and I chased those things with the same enthusiasm that I gave to my music. By the time I was 22, I had it all—except fame and success.

Giving my life to Jesus changed everything. As I said before, the night I got saved and Sherri and I got remarried, we both walked out of that church addiction-free. I could hardly believe what Jesus had done for me. He had forgiven my sins, given me eternal life, cleaned me up, and made me sober—all at the same time. It seemed too good to be true. In fact, to be perfectly honest, I went home that night wondering if I would feel the same way in the morning. Something truly amazing had happened to me—a "God thing"—and it was real and lasting.

Getting saved brought other changes, too. I grew up in the Kansas City-Liberty, Missouri area, so I was pretty much a city boy. Not long after I was saved, however, Sherri, Jason, and I moved to the country and invested our lives in that little country church where I had found Jesus. We were happy, we loved Jesus, we had a great church family, and our marriage and family life were better and stronger and happier than I would ever have dreamed possible. Everything was great—for awhile.

Eventually, over a long period of time, the leadership in that little church became very cynical and self-protecting in attitude. I'm not saying this to be judgmental or critical of any individuals; I'm just stating a fact. A sweet spirit of openness and simple love and fellowship in following Jesus transitioned gradually into an atmosphere that demanded or expected "performance." In other words, liberty in Jesus gave way to religious legalism.

Trapped in "Performance" Mode

One of the personal consequences of this change was the initial suppression of my dream. I had to make a choice: I could follow Jesus or I could play my rock music, but I could not do both. So, in order to keep the peace and conform to the expectations of Christians I respected and regarded as more mature and more knowledgable than I, I "gave up" my dream. As a young and growing Christian still learning the matters of the Spirit, I didn't know any better. I was spiritually naïve. In my heart I gave up my rock music willingly "as unto the Lord" because I thought that was what I was supposed to do to be a "good" Christian. In the end, all I did was smother my God-given dream, but I didn't realize it at the time.

All in all, we stayed in that church 16 years, and for the most part, they were good years. God blessed us, we grew in the Lord, and Sherri and I raised our two kids there. For eight years I owned a computer software business. The only reason I gave it up was to go into full-time ministry.

By the early 1990s I was sensing a growing yearning in my heart to reach people for Christ. I began to realize that the Holy Spirit had given me the gift of evangelism and I became eager for opportunities to exercise it. Because our church did not believe in "promotion" of any type, I started praying and before long began receiving invitations to preach. This made some of the church leadership nervous. When I tried to get the church to look at its image, they began to perceive me as a "threat." And so began a three-year period of "transition."

Sometime during this period I attended a friend's church where 70 people responded to accept Jesus as Savior in *one* service! It totally freaked me out. The evangelist in me leapt for joy. This was how the gospel was supposed to work! In 1993 Sherri, the kids, and I moved to this church and I joined its ministry staff. The church at that time was one of the fastest growing churches in America in a city of 79,000.

Before long, I became assistant pastor with the responsibility of administering a five million dollar new church construction project. In addition, I also oversaw the "crisis" ministries: staff problems, congregational problems, counseling, and personal ministry. Sherri handled all the hospital visitation. Needless to say, with all of these responsibilities in a rapidly-growing church, my dreams once again took a backseat.

But hey, it wasn't so bad, was it? After all, I was successful, I was serving the Lord, and our church was reaching people for Jesus. My marriage was great, my kids were super; what more could a man ask for? Life was a dream, right? It certainly was. It just wasn't *my* dream.

By 1998 I was beginning to feel discontented. Outwardly everything was fine. The church was growing, I had a successful and respected ministry, and my family life was peaceful, stable, and emotionally fulfilling. When we came to the church in 1993 we were the right people for the right time, but I knew now that I had to make a change. Something just wasn't right with me.

For some reason I didn't connect my unrest with my dreams, so I started looking elsewhere. Reflecting back on all my years in church and in ministry experience, I realized I had a great résumé. *I could pastor a church of my own*, I thought. In December 1998 I sat down with my friend and pastor, shared my feelings of discontent and told him I thought it was time for us to move on. He was very sympathetic to my dilemma and we talked for quite awhile. In fact, in the end we talked ourselves out of making any changes.

Things continued as they were for the next several months but the heaviness in my heart continued to grow. By September 1999 I had reached the point where I knew it was time to make a change. Nothing was wrong in the church or the ministry or in my relations with any of the staff or the congregation. It's just that something was wrong with me. One day my pastor saw me in the sanctuary and asked me how I was doing. I looked at him and said, "I can't do this anymore."

This time there was no discussion. He understood where I was and graciously offered to assist me in making a smooth transition. He helped me look for a church to pastor. I put out feelers and submitted résumés—but nothing happened. As the days and weeks passed I grew more and more frustrated. We had established March 1, 2000, as a "drop-dead" date to leave no matter what, and it was fast approaching. For weeks Sherri and I had been praying and seeking the Lord and trying to discern where we were to go and what we were to do, but we never got a sense of peace about any particular direction.

Ready to Go But Where?

Finally, in February 2000 the answer came. One weekend I preached at a church in Mississippi and the pastor said to me later, "You will know tomorrow what you are to do." I took it as a word from the Lord. Sure enough, the next day, somewhere between

Jackson, Mississippi, and Memphis, Tennessee, we decided to start traveling.

The prospect was scary and exciting all at the same time. We had never done anything like this before (even though I had dreamed of this very thing for years). Such a venture as this was full of all sorts of questions, variables, and unknowns. How do we even begin such a project? Would we get enough invitations to make this whole thing viable? Would we be able to survive financially? What if we were making a mistake? Were we ready for this?

Dreams and risk go hand in hand.

Without a doubt, it would have been "safer" to stay with what was familiar, but people who always insist on "playing it safe" rarely fulfill their dreams. Dreams and risk go hand in hand. For years I had smothered my dream in the name of "religion" to the point where it had almost died. Years of living to meet others' expectations and serving others' dreams had almost been fatal to my own. Now I had a chance to pursue and fulfill *my* dream, the dream God had planted in *my* heart as a child, and I sensed somehow that if I didn't do this it might be my last opportunity. It was as though God was saying to me, "Here it is; here's your chance to realize your dream. What are you going to do with it?" I decided to take the plunge. It was now or never. Sure, it was an act of faith. The Bible says that we walk by faith and not by sight, which means we trust the Lord to guide our way even when we can't see the path. I stepped out in faith—and there was no turning back.

Invitations to minister started coming in from different churches and prisons. I would go in with my guitar and sing a couple of songs before preaching— and God would show up. As word got out, more invitations followed. The doors opened for me to go into prisons and sing and preach about Jesus. In April 2001 I went to Macon, Georgia, to record my first CD, *Honey in the Rock*. Then I had the chance to put together my own band of great musicians— something I'd dreamed of all my life—and we began doing some concerts together.

A pastor in Kansas City insisted that we do a blues concert at his church—*on a Sunday morning!* I told him he was crazy, but he still insisted. At the time I wondered, *Will anybody come to church to hear blues?* It went great; the place was packed. Since then, "Blues Sundays" have become a regular part of our ministry.

Once, in Mountain Home, Arkansas, while doing a Blues Sunday, the church scheduled us to play at a place called the Top Hat Lounge. This opened my eyes to the fact that God could take us into a secular environment and through our music reach people right where they live. Today, we get all sorts of gigs to take our music into secular venues.

It's been five years since Sherri and I decided to follow our dreams and, except for finding Jesus, it's the best thing I've ever done. The shackles came off and the "wild man" that is the *true* Jimmie Bratcher was released and set loose on the world. Never in my life have I been as fulfilled, satisfied, healthy, happy, and in tune with my destiny as I am today because I know I am doing what God created me to do. This is His calling on my life and I wouldn't want to be doing anything else. I'm fulfilling the dreams of my life. I won't take my dreams to the grave. I don't intend to leave this life with unfulfilled and unexpressed dreams. I intend to die empty.

I've taken time to tell you my story for two reasons. First, even though today I am living and fulfilling my life's dream, it might never have happened. I came close to smothering my dream to the point of no return, and I don't want the same thing to happen to you. Second, I want to encourage you that it's never too late to follow your dream. If I can pursue and fulfill my life's dream, then you can, too.

PERSONAL DREAM JOURNAL

CHAPTER FOUR

What's Holding You Back?

Everybody has a dream, including you. The problem is that so few people ever see their dreams come to pass. Personal or financial setbacks, family tragedies, the practical demands of everyday living, and other "realities" of life cause them to suppress or submerge their dreams, often forever.

A dream can remain suppressed for only so long before it starts trying to reassert itself. When that happens, feelings of discontent arise. On the surface things may seem fine—even great—but underneath runs an undercurrent of growing unrest, a suspicion that something somewhere is just not right. Does that describe you? Do you suspect that something is missing in your life or that somehow you are missing out on something you are supposed to be doing, even if externally everything seems to be fine? Do you feel a discontent or an unrest that you can't quite put your finger on? Maybe a dream you have smothered is struggling to rise to the surface again.

What's holding you back? What personal dreams have *you* suppressed for the sake of public opinion or expectations? What aspirations have you put on hold to help fulfill someone else's dream? This is not necessarily a bad thing. Working for the dreams of others is valuable training and preparation time for us before we launch out in pursuit of our own goals. It may be that serving someone else's dreams and vision *is* your dream, and if that is your dream, it is an honorable one. But if not, you have to take a deep breath, take the plunge, and go after your own dreams.

Religion Can Steal Our Dreams

There are many things in life that can steal our dreams. With little doubt, *religion* is one of the main culprits. There's no telling how many dreams have been stolen, suppressed, and lost over the years for the sake of conformity to religious expectations. When I say "religion," I'm not talking about a relationship with Jesus, but man-made rules and rituals that have very little to do with the things of God and everything to do with human pride.

Jesus encountered this kind of prideful religious attitude in the Pharisees and other religious leaders of His day, and He was very plain and outspoken about it:

> *But woe to you, scribes and Pharisees, hypocrites! For you shut up the kingdom of heaven against men; for you neither go in yourselves, nor do you allow those who are entering to go in. Woe to you, scribes and Pharisees, hypocrites! For you devour widows' houses, and for a pretense make long prayers. Therefore you will receive greater condemnation* (Matthew 23:13–14).

The Gospels contain many other examples, but I chose these verses because they seem to touch on people's dreams. Who doesn't dream of entering the kingdom of Heaven? Yet the scribes and Pharisees, by their religious demands and hypocritical lifestyles, prevented others from going in. In other words, those who sincerely wanted to enter God's kingdom had that dream stolen by the hypocrisy of a man-based religious system. And what about the "widows' houses"? Doesn't a house represent someone's dreams? Apparently, some of the Pharisees were landlords or moneylenders who had no compunctions about foreclosing even on poor widows, leaving them out on the street.

Religion is one of the biggest dream stealers of all.

Similar attitudes exist with many people today. Even if they are not written down anywhere (sometimes they are), rules and expectations still exist regarding dress, behavior, appearance, "acceptable" music, or recreation or other activities, and on and on and on. None of these rules are based on the Bible but on some person's idea of what makes somebody a "good Christian." Religion is one of the biggest dream stealers of all.

Have you lost touch with your dream because of trying to meet the unreasonable expectations of a religious system? Then it is time to make a change, isn't it?

Other Dream Stealers

Dreams can also fall prey to financial realities. Just think of the countless young men and women whose dreams of college and a bright, successful career and future have been dashed because they lacked the financial resources to make it happen. Some dreams cost money to fulfill—sometimes a lot of money. Dream fulfillment generally involves a certain amount of risk. Pursuing a dream means shooting for the stars, swinging for the fence which always carries the risk of failure. Many people are not willing to take that risk. Instead, they opt for the security of a regular paycheck, working for someone else while sidelining their own dream.

Are you postponing your dream because you don't know how you would pay for it? If yes, then don't let that stop you.

Health issues can also put a damper on dream fulfillment. We've all heard stories of young adult children having to put their educations or careers on hold in order to deal with sudden or unexpected health problems in their parents. Sometimes a health issue can seemingly stop the dream pursuit dead in its tracks. Consider the up-and-coming painter or photographer who goes blind or the champion swimmer paralyzed in a diving accident.

Is there a health issue in your life or in the life of a loved one that is holding you back from pursuing your dream? Don't give up. Nothing is impossible with God. No matter what obstacle may seem to be in your path, your dream can still come to pass. In getting there, however, God may lead you down a different path than you anticipated, but His way is always sure.

Family responsibilities such as supporting and raising children often lead to dream postponement. This is particularly true in cases of unwed and/or teen pregnancies. Just ask any young mother or father who has struggled to finish school or get ahead career-wise with an unexpected baby added to the mix. For many couples, of course, raising a family is their dream, and what a fantastic dream! They deliberately put their personal dreams on a back burner while they raise their kids. Then, after the kids are grown and on their own, they pull their dreams off the shelf, blow the dust off, and go after them. That really is what happened to Sherri and me, and it is something we will never regret.

Have you sidelined your dream because of family responsibilities?

Dreams may also die over the issue of education or, more often, the lack of it. Let's face it, some dreams, particularly many professional dreams, require a high level of formal education, and that requirement presents a formidable barrier for many people. Financial hardship, learning disabilities, and family obligations are just a few of the factors that can stand in the way of a person receiving the education needed to fulfill a dream.

Are you holding up on a personal dream because you lack the necessary education?

Perhaps the greatest dream stealer of all is *fear.* Many people are simply too scared to take the risk involved in pursuing their dream. They're afraid they might fail, so they don't even try. Sometimes they have been convinced by friends or family that their dream is too big or too risky or too costly or simply just out of their league. They have come to believe what others have told them—that they lack the intelligence or the skills or the drive or the vision to go after what they want. So, instead of doing it anyway and proving everybody wrong, they play it safe and never discover who they really are or what they were really capable of. In other words, they never release the potential God put inside them.

Are you allowing fear to smother your dream?

Your Dreams Are God-Given

Obstacles to dream fulfillment are very real; I don't deny that. At the same time, however, I believe that

49

ultimately no obstacle is insurmountable, especially if you desire your dream strongly enough. Thomas Edison received very little formal education and was a poor student. In spite of this, as well as the fact that he suffered from severe deafness, he went on to become one of the most brilliant and prolific inventors in our nation's history, counting among his many achievements the light bulb, the phonograph, and motion-picture photography.

In 1981, pilot and mountain climber Ed Hommer lost the bottom portions of both legs due to frostbite after surviving a plane crash on Mount McKinley in Alaska and five days in a winter storm. Despite this setback, he returned to flying, becoming the first double amputee to receive a medical certification to fly commercial airliners. He also resumed mountain climbing. In 1999, he returned to the site of his original injuries and became the first double amputee to climb Mount McKinley, the tallest peak in North America. In 2001 he sought to become the first legless climber to climb Mount Everest, but bad weather forced him and his team to turn back only 3,000 feet from the summit. Ed Hommer loved flying and he loved mountain climbing and he didn't allow the loss of his legs to prevent him from pursuing either dream.

Thomas Edison and Ed Hommer fulfilled their dreams because their desire was greater than the obstacles they faced. The strength of their vision kept them going against all odds, and they succeeded.

Desire is extremely important when it comes to fulfilling our dreams, but there is another factor that is even more significant, particularly for Christians: the guiding hand of God.

What is your dream? What is the greatest desire of your heart? Whatever it is, you need to understand that God put it there.

What is your dream? What is the greatest desire of your heart? Whatever it is, you need to understand that God put it there. He didn't take it away when you got saved. Your dream is God-given and because God gave it to you, He wants to see you fulfill it. God has placed inside each of us incredible potential and His desire is to see that potential unleashed so we can live the abundant life Jesus came to give us and become everything we can be in Him.

The apostle Paul had a significant barrier to overcome in order to achieve his dream: he was a

Pharisee. Once Paul came to Christ, before he could become the dynamic apostle and missionary God had called him to be, he had to lay aside his pride in his Jewish heritage and his great knowledge and move forward to fulfill his calling and potential in Christ. He described his experience this way:

> *But whatever things were gain to me, those things I have counted as loss for the sake of Christ. More than that, I count all things to be loss in view of the surpassing value of knowing Christ Jesus my Lord, for whom I have suffered the loss of all things, and count them but rubbish so that I may gain Christ, and may be found in Him, not having a righteousness of my own derived from the Law, but that which is through faith in Christ, the righteousness which comes from God on the basis of faith, that I may know Him and the power of His resurrection and the fellowship of His sufferings, being conformed to His death; in order that I may attain to the resurrection from the dead.*
>
> *Not that I have already obtained it or have already become perfect, but I press on so that I may lay hold of that for which also I was laid hold of by Christ Jesus. Brethren, I do not regard*

myself as having laid hold of it yet; but one thing
I do: forgetting what lies behind and reaching
forward to what lies ahead, I press on toward
the goal for the prize of the upward call of God
in Christ Jesus (Philippians 3:7–14 NASB).

Paul was determined that nothing, not even his impressive ethnic and intellectual credentials, was going to prevent him from realizing his dream.

God wants you to fulfill your dream. In fact, He wants to fulfill it in and through you. As a Christian, you have the fullness of God dwelling in you through the Holy Spirit. This means that you have all the resources of God available to help you fulfill the dream that He planted in your heart.

Sure, it's risky. Pursuing your dream always carries risks, but so does anything else in this world that is worth doing. Genesis chapter 12 tells how Abram left his homeland and his father's house to go to a land that he had never seen before. His reason? God told him to go and promised to bless him and to make his descendents into a great nation. Risky? Of course, by any ordinary human standard. But Abram had the promise of God's presence with him wherever he went.

As a Christian, you have that same promise. If the dream you have harbored in your heart for so many years is beginning to stir once more, it may be God's way of telling you that it's time to go for it. Don't smother it. Pursuing your dream will connect you with God's dream and desire for you:

> *"For I know the plans that I have for you," declares the Lord, "plans for welfare and not for calamity to give you a future and a hope"* (Jeremiah 29:11 NASB).

God wants you to succeed in your dream but He wants you to do so in conjunction with an ongoing relationship of love and obedience with Him. He offers this promise to all dream-seekers:

> *Delight yourself in the Lord; and He will give you the desires of your heart* (Psalm 37:4 NASB).

Don't let your dream die. Search deep inside yourself and draw out that "wild man," that dreamer you almost forgot was there, and let him go. After all, you have a great precedent: Jesus Christ the Son of God—the *original* "wild man."

CHAPTER FIVE

Jesus the "Wild Man"

Jesus is a wild man; a wild Savior. He blew into the culture of His day preaching that the kingdom of Heaven was at hand and turned the society of His day—and especially its religious culture—upside-down. Perhaps I should say He turned it right-side-up because it was the religious leaders of the day with their false legalism and obsessive focus on works who had overturned the faith of Israel's forefathers and replaced it with empty religion.

Practically everything about Jesus was radical and provocative for the society through which He walked: the things He said, the kind of people He hung out with, where He came from (Galilee, the "sticks" of that area), and even His personal background (it was rumored that He was conceived out of wedlock).

One of the wildest and most radical things about Jesus was His single-minded focus on love and acceptance toward everyone in a society steeped in selfishness and class-consciousness. After all, this is the man who described His work on earth with these words:

> *The Spirit of the Lord is upon Me, because He has anointed Me to preach the gospel to the poor; He has sent Me to heal the brokenhearted, to proclaim liberty to the captives and recovery of sight to the blind, to set at liberty those who are oppressed; to proclaim the acceptable year of the Lord* (Luke 4:18–19).

Jesus is also the man who said that the two greatest commandments—the two most important things we can do—are to love God with all our heart, soul, mind, and strength, and to love our neighbor as ourselves. Jesus went even further than this. When common custom said, "Love your neighbor and hate your enemy," Jesus said we should love our enemies also and pray for them. Jesus wanted everyone to know the love of God and He displayed that love in everything He said and did. That in itself was radical.

Comforting the Afflicted

Sometimes "wild men" comfort the afflicted. Jesus certainly did this on countless occasions when He healed the sick, forgave sins, and raised the dead. Think of the woman with an issue of blood who had found no relief for 12 years and who, hearing that Jesus was nearby, made her way through the crowd and touched His clothing. Instantly she was healed. Jesus looked at her and said, "Daughter, your faith has made you well. Go in peace, and be healed of your affliction" (Mark 5:34).

And what about the widow of Nain who had just lost her only son and her only means of support? As she left the city with her son's funeral procession, Jesus approached and said to her, "Do not weep." Then He brought her son back to life (see Luke 7:11–15).

Don't forget Bartimaeus, a blind beggar of Jericho who called out loudly to Jesus for healing. Even as the crowd around Bartimaeus tried to silence him, Jesus called him forward and restored his sight (see Mark 10:46–52).

Then, of course, there's Jairus, a synagogue leader whose 12-year-old daughter was dying. He asked Jesus to heal her but on the way to the house received the news that the girl had just died. Jesus said, "Do not be afraid; only believe, and she will be made well." Arriving at the house, Jesus permitted only the girl's parents and His three closest disciples—Peter, James, and John—to enter. Jesus took the girl by the hand and said, "Little girl, arise." She did. (See Luke 8:41–42, 49–56.)

Jesus was a "wild man" in that He always showed love, mercy, and acceptance to everyone who came to Him, regardless of their status in society or of the social customs of the day, especially when those customs got in the way of mercy and ministry. Jesus readily entered the home of Zacchaeus, a despised and ostracized tax collector who needed the touch of God's grace. Jesus was accused (and "guilty") of eating with "tax gatherers and sinners" whom the self-righteous would have nothing to do with. On one of those occasions, Jesus even welcomed the love gestures of a "fallen" woman who anointed His head with expensive oil and wiped

Jesus was a "wild man" in that He always showed love, mercy, and acceptance to everyone who came to Him.

His feet with her hair. And, in a society that regarded women as second-class citizens (only a little higher than slaves), Jesus readily welcomed women as followers and equals.

One day a crowd brought before Jesus a woman who had been caught in the act of adultery. The Jewish law stated that she should be stoned but the crowd, testing Jesus, asked Him what should be done. Jesus said, "He who is without sin among you, let him throw a stone at her first" (John 8:7). As the woman's accusers melted away in silence, Jesus spoke to the woman:

> *"Woman, where are those accusers of yours? Has no one condemned you?"*
>
> *She said, "No one, Lord."*
>
> *And Jesus said to her, "Neither do I condemn you; go and sin no more"* (John 8:10–11).

Jesus was a "wild man," a radical who openly displayed to everyone He met the radical love, grace, and mercy of God.

Jesus: A "Meek" Wild Man?

Just because Jesus was a wild man does not mean He was out of control. No more self-controlled person has ever walked the face of the earth than Jesus. But how can a person be "wild" and self-controlled at the same time? It all depends on the kind of wildness we're talking about. Twice in the New Testament Jesus is described by a Greek word that means "meek." In Matthew 11:29 Jesus says of Himself, "Take My yoke upon you, and learn of Me; for I am *meek* and lowly in heart: and ye shall find rest unto your souls" (KJV emphasis added). Matthew 21:5, quoting Zechariah 9:9 and applying it to Jesus says, "Tell ye the daughter of Sion, Behold, thy King cometh unto thee, *meek*, and sitting upon an ass, and a colt the foal of an ass" (KJV emphasis added).

To our modern ears, the word "meek" has negative connotations of weakness and submissiveness. A meek person is someone who never asserts himself and allows others to walk over him and take advantage of him. In fact, one definition of "meek" is "deficient in spirit and courage." That certainly does *not* describe Jesus! No one deficient in spirit and courage would have dared to accept the "unacceptable," touch the "untouchable," and love the "unlovable" as openly and as freely as Jesus did. Who would have been attracted to someone who was completely submissive and unassertive?

Yet thousands were drawn to Jesus by the dynamic nature of His life and His words, not to mention His gentle spirit of compassion in healing the sick.

It is in the word "gentle" that we begin to get at the heart of what it means to be wild and yet self-controlled. Most modern English versions of the Bible use the word "gentle" instead of the word "meek" in Matthew 11:29 and 21:5. The biblical word refers primarily to a temper of spirit and attitude toward God of accepting His dealings as good without disputing or resisting. In this sense it matches a lesser-known modern usage of "meek" as meaning to endure injury with patience and without resentment. Jesus displayed this attitude of meekness (gentleness) when from the cross He said, "Father, forgive them, for they do not know what they do" (Luke 23:34).

Part of the problem in understanding the meekness of Jesus is due to the fact that no English word can adequately translate the Greek word with the full force and meaning that it contains. For many today, the words "meek" and "gentle" suggest weakness and submissiveness to some degree or another, but meekness in the sense of the Greek word used in the New Testament was a fruit of *power* not weakness. We often tend to think of a meek person as being unable to help himself. Jesus, however, was meek because He had all the resources of God at His command, yet He was in complete control at all times. Rather than weakness, then, the meekness or gentleness of Jesus demonstrated *strength under control.*

The same Greek word was used to describe a horse that had been broken to accept a rider. Breaking a horse does not break its spirit or weaken it in any way. It is just as strong as it was before, only now its strength (wildness) has been brought under control. The strength and wildness are still there; they have just been channeled in a specific direction.

Rather than weakness, then, the meekness or gentleness of Jesus demonstrated strength under control.

In *The Chronicles of Narnia*, his popular fantasy series, C. S. Lewis points out the "wildness" of Jesus; His "strength under control." The character Aslan, the great lion, represents Christ in the stories and the reader as well as the characters are informed early on that while Aslan is benevolent, he is not a "tame" lion. Despite his gentleness and benevolence, Aslan is *still* wild.

So how could Jesus be a "wild man" and self-controlled at the same time? Because His self-control was *strength* under control. As the Son of God, Jesus had all the resources and power of Heaven at His disposal yet He chose to walk in humble submission to His Father's will, even to His death on the cross. Jesus did not die because He was weak and had no choice; He died because that was the will of His Father and He chose to walk that path. No one who ever encountered Jesus, friend or foe, came away believing that He was weak. Had He been weak, His enemies could have dismissed Him as harmless. It was His very strength and power that threatened them to the point of plotting to kill Him.

This "meekness" or strength under control is the same quality Jesus was referring to when He said, "Blessed are the meek, for they shall inherit the earth" (Matthew 5:5). Who will inherit the earth? Not the meek in the sense of the weak, spiritless, cowardly types who whine and complain at the slightest inconvenience, hurt, or injustice or who sue at the drop of a hat. The inheritors of the earth will be the meek who are "wild" people under self-control, people who exhibit gentleness with an undercurrent of strength. Being meek doesn't mean sacrificing our wildness.

Released to Be Wild

So often people come to Jesus and after they are saved they get channeled into one church or another where they are taught to lay aside their "wild side" and become good little Christians who never offend anybody. They never fulfill their dreams or reach their potential, and therefore, never do much of anything for Christ and His kingdom.

That's not how Jesus operated. In all the personal encounters that Jesus had with people for healing or deliverance, never once did He "tame" the people. Never once did He remove their wild spirit or tell them to squelch their dream in order to conform to the status quo. Jesus was a wild man and He wanted to release the true wildness in others so that they would be free to become themselves the way God intended.

The Gospel of Mark provides a classic example of how Jesus operated this way:

Then they came to the other side of the sea, to the country of the Gadarenes. And when He had come out of the boat, immediately there met Him out of the tombs a man with an unclean spirit, who had his dwelling among the tombs; and no one could bind him, not even with chains, because he had often been bound with shackles and chains. And the chains had been pulled apart by him, and the shackles broken in pieces; neither could anyone tame him. And always, night and day, he was in the mountains and in the tombs, crying out and cutting himself with stones (Mark 5:1–5).

Here's an interesting scene: Jesus and His disciples are on the east side of the Sea of Galilee, in non-Jewish territory. No sooner has He stepped out of the boat than Jesus, the self-controlled "wild man," meets another "wild man" who is completely out of control. No one could restrain him. In fact, it says specifically that no one could "tame" him. He had broken every chain and every shackle with which he had been bound until the local populace apparently gave up, abandoning him to wander among the tombs. His formidable strength and power were useless, dissipated by the unrestrained madness that was caused by the demonic presence in him.

When he saw Jesus from afar, he ran and worshiped Him. And he cried out with a loud voice and said, "What have I to do with You, Jesus, Son of the Most High God? I implore

You by God that You do not torment me."

For He said to him, "Come out of the man, unclean spirit!" Then He asked him, "What is your name?" And he answered, saying, "My name is Legion; for we are many." Also he begged Him earnestly that He would not send them out of the country (Mark 5:6–10).

Notice that the evil spirits in this man recognized Jesus right off the bat. As fallen angels and former residents of Heaven themselves, they knew the Son of God when they saw Him. There was no mistaking the aura of divine authority that emanated from Jesus. They were terrified at the arrival of this divine "wild man" of whose wildness their own (which they had unleashed in the Gadarene man) was only a warped and corrupted copy.

Now a large herd of swine was feeding there near the mountains. So all the demons begged Him, saying, "Send us to the swine, that we may enter them." And at once Jesus gave them permission. Then the unclean spirits went out and entered the swine (there were about two thousand); and the herd ran violently down the steep place into the sea, and drowned in the sea.

So those who fed the swine fled, and they told it in the city and in the country. And they went out to see what it was that had happened. Then they came to Jesus, and saw the one who had been demon-possessed and had the legion, sitting and clothed and in his right mind. And they were afraid. And those who saw it told them how it happened to him who had been demon-possessed, and about the swine. Then they began to plead with Him to depart from their region (Mark 5:11–17).

How many demons would it take to possess an entire herd of swine? One demon per pig? No one knows. All we know is that there were *many* demons possessing this Gadarene wild man. As soon as they departed him at Jesus' command and entered the pigs, the entire herd went wild and drowned themselves in the sea. That's where uncontrolled wildness will lead you. Before I was saved, the uncontrolled wildness of alcohol and drugs and everything else in my life could easily have led to my death at any time. Today, the alcohol and drugs are gone, but the wildness is not. Now I'm just wild for Jesus.

After his deliverance, the Gadarene man was clothed and in his right mind, and the sight of it, plus the account told by the swine herders, terrified the local people. Apparently, they couldn't take wildness in any form. They asked Jesus to leave! Can you imagine that? What an opportunity they missed! Maybe they were afraid He would make *them* mad so they would drown themselves in the sea!

> And when He got into the boat, he who had been demon-possessed begged Him that he might be with Him. However, Jesus did not permit him, but said to him, "Go home to your friends, and tell them what great things the Lord has done for you, and how He has had compassion on you." And he departed and began to proclaim in Decapolis all that Jesus had done for him; and all marveled (Mark 5:18–20).

Here's the most important part of the story. The Gadarene man, newly delivered from demonic possession, wanted to stay with Jesus, but Jesus had something else in mind. Instead, Jesus told him to go home and tell all his friends what the Lord had done for him. Immediately the man began to "proclaim in Decapolis all that Jesus has done for him." The word "Decapolis" means "ten cities" and referred to a geographic region of ten Gentile cities south and east of the Sea of Galilee that were linked by culture and political alliance.

Unless this man had a whole lot of friends and had gotten around a whole lot before his days of possession and madness, he went far beyond Jesus' instruction to "go home to your friends and tell them." Apparently, once he started talking about Jesus, he couldn't stop and went all over the "ten cities" region telling everybody he met about the wonder and compassion of the Lord. In other words, he "went wild" with his witness. He was still a wild man, only now, like me, he was a wild man for Jesus.

He doesn't want us to go through our lives with our natural, real, wild person locked up inside unable to express itself.

Jesus delivered this man from the legion of demons that had possessed him, but He did not deliver him from his wildness. Instead, Jesus *released* his wildness. Before, the man's wildness was unrestrained, under the so-called "control" of the demons. Once freed from their influence, he was released to bring his natural wildness under his own control and channel it for better and more prosperous uses. No one knows who this man was or what he did before. Perhaps at one time he had been a successful merchant or a prosperous landowner. His possession and unrestrained wildness robbed him of his life and his dreams. Jesus restored them. Rather than suppressing the man's wildness, Jesus released it and liberated him to become *himself* once more; in fact, more himself than he had ever been before.

That's what Jesus wants for all of us. He doesn't want us to go through our lives with our natural, real, wild person locked up inside unable to express itself. He is a wild man and He wants us to be wild men (and women) too because that is part of our nature as God created us. We don't have to fear the wild part of ourselves or be afraid of how God is going to respond. God will be delighted. After all, God *loves* wild people!

CHAPTER SIX

God Loves Wild People

God loves wild people and Jesus proved it. Jesus went where nobody of "decent" standing would go. He frequented the houses and gathering places of all sorts of sinners, untouchables, and "lowlifes": prostitutes, tax collectors, adulterers, and adulteresses, the sick, the dirty, the destitute; anybody and everybody whom those in "proper" society had written off as worthless and cursed by God.

These are the very people Jesus focused on in His ministry and He was sharply criticized and condemned for it, particularly by the religious leaders and elite of the day. Did that bother Jesus? Not on your life. As a wild man who loved wild people, Jesus was not concerned about His reputation among the hypocrites and those who put on false airs of superiority. He was too busy loving the unlovely and drawing in the outcasts to tell them and, more importantly, *show* them how much God loved them. Jesus was too busy redeeming the lost to be concerned about the opinions of people who couldn't be bothered with the plight of those less fortunate than themselves. Jesus did not just reach out to the down-and-outers; He also ministered to the up-and-outers as well.

Where have we gone wrong? How have we gotten so far off base from Jesus' example? Let's be honest. Generally speaking, do we do any better of a job seeking out and having compassion on the poor and needy and outcasts of our day than did the scribes and Pharisees of Jesus' day? Often we are so quick to judge their pride and arrogance and insensitivity, but are we really any better? Don't we prefer the company of others like ourselves to associating with the "great unwashed"? Isn't it easier just to pray or send money than to get our hands dirty or endanger our reputation? "What will people think if I do that?"

We need to return to our wild roots. We have a wild Savior. Our Leader is a wild man and He wants us to follow His example. We are His people and are therefore wild people also. After all, when we received Jesus by faith we were given the mind of

Christ (see 1 Corinthians 2:16) and are destined to be conformed to His image (see Romans 8:29). This means that if Jesus is a wild man, we are wild people as well, and we are supposed to live and act as He did. Our calling is to go into all the world and find other wild people who, like the Gadarene demoniac, need to have their wildness brought under the light and direction of Christ, not to tame it but to release it so they can pursue their dreams in the manner God always intended.

I love to watch as God does what He does with people and especially with people whom most of us normally wouldn't expect God to work with: wild people. It just thrills my heart to stand back and watch God restore a marriage or deliver an addict or save someone's soul. Those are the things that crank me up and get my motor running. Did you recognize that quote from the song "Born to Be Wild"? "Get your motor running, head out on the highway!" That's what we need to be doing as followers of Jesus. There are lots of wild people just waiting to be introduced to Jesus, the ultimate wild man.

A Wild God Works with Wild People

God loves wild people because He is a wild God. That's why Jesus was a wild man: like Father like

Son. What's that? You don't think God is wild? Think again. The God of the Bible is a far cry from the tame, comfortable, inoffensive, and undemanding version we encounter in so many churches. Who but a wild God would appear to Moses in a burning bush? Who but a wild God would manifest Himself to the nation of Israel as a pillar of cloud by day and a pillar of fire by night? Who but a wild God would announce His presence on the mountain by thunder and lightning? Who but the wild Son of a wild God would be referred to (as Jesus is) as the "Lion of the tribe of Judah"? (See Revelation 5:5.)

Yes, God is wild and He loves wild people.

Yes, God is wild and He loves wild people. He also loves to work with wild people. Even a casual examination of the Bible reveals that God chose all sorts of people to work with to carry out His purposes. Many times when I am ministering in prisons I think about Moses and David who were both murderers, and yet God used them. That is simply too wild for many people to understand. But it's great news for inmates who realize that no matter how much they have messed up their lives, it's never too late for God to help them and use them. That's one of the things I love so much about the Lord: He shows no partiality. No one is beyond the reach of His saving grace and transforming power.

Moses: A Wild Man

Let's look a little closer at Moses. He was a wild man, too. Oh sure, he was raised in the house of Pharaoh and received a fine education and lessons in deportment and royal bearing in the finest tradition of the Egyptians. Moses was being groomed as Egyptian royalty, but his natural wildness was never tamed; it simply went into hiding under the veneer of his civilized upbringing.

That wildness reappeared one day when Moses was 40. Throughout his years in Pharaoh's house Moses never forgot his heritage as a Hebrew. One day Moses saw an Egyptian beating a Hebrew slave. Enraged, Moses killed the Egyptian and buried the body. Already, the heart of a deliverer was showing itself in Moses, but the time was not right. In short order Moses had to flee for his life into the desert of Midian where he spent the next 40 years as a shepherd while God focused his wild heart and nature into the deliverer and national leader he was destined to be.

Moses became a wild man for God, returning to Pharaoh and going head-to-head with him and his magicians and sorcerers who consistently came out on the short end of the stick. Throughout the rest of his life Moses led the Israelites in the wilderness, a wild man who was never tamed, but whose wildness was shaped and directed by the wild God he loved and served.

King David: A Wild Man

Then there's David. Although he was Israel's greatest king, this wild man started out as a shepherd keeping the flocks of his father, Jesse. In the fields of his home is where David got to know the wild God of the flocks and fields and the heavens. The relationship forged there carried David all his life. The Bible describes David as a man after God's own heart, and yet he was an adulterer and a murderer. David's adultery with Bathsheba resulted in a pregnancy. Efforts to cover up that sin led to the murder of Bathsheba's husband, Uriah, one of David's best generals. David then married Bathsheba.

When David was confronted with the magnitude of his sin he repented and received God's forgiveness, thus demonstrating the true nature of his heart as one after God's own heart. Despite his sins and personal flaws, which were many, David loved God wildly and passionately. Throughout his reign as king of Israel, David never lost his wild edge, or his wild love for God, and God promised that one of David's descendants would rule forever. King David of the tribe of Judah thus became a physical ancestor of Jesus Christ, the "Lion of the tribe of Judah," and the ultimate "wild man."

Paul: A Wild Man

One of the truly wild men of the New Testament was the apostle Paul. The first time we meet Paul (then known as Saul) he is looking on with approval while holding the coats of the men who are stoning to death Stephen, the first follower of Jesus to be killed for his faith. A short time later we see Saul as a wild man for God, at least God as Saul saw Him through the lenses of a strict, legalistic Pharisee. Saul zealously and even eagerly persecuted the early followers of Jesus, branding them heretics and blasphemers, and dragging them into jail whenever and wherever he could find them. He didn't even wait for them to show themselves; Saul actively pursued them. In all of this he thought he was serving and pleasing God.

While on the road from Jerusalem to Damascus on just such a mission, Saul encountered Jesus in a blinding vision of light, an encounter that transformed Saul's life forever. Having given his life to Christ, Paul, as he now became known, became an ardent defender and advocate of the faith he had so vigorously attacked before. Someone once said that Paul did not become a fanatic when he became a Christian. Paul was *always* a fanatic; he just switched sides. In the 30-some years between his conversion on the Damascus road and his execution in Rome by order of Nero, this fanatical wild man of Jesus was the prime force behind carrying the message of Christ to all parts of the Roman Empire. Almost at the very end of his life, Paul said, "I have fought the good fight, I have finished the race, I have kept the faith" (2 Timothy 4:7).

> *Paul did not become a fanatic when he became a Christian. Paul was always a fanatic; he just switched sides.*

Paul's dream was to serve Jesus faithfully and see as many people as possible come to faith in Jesus. He pursued this dream with every ounce of energy he possessed. It was the single focus of his life. His example can be an encouragement to all of us as we pursue the dreams God has given us. Remember, our past doesn't matter. What matters is starting where we are and moving steadily toward the future God has for us. Paul said it like this:

But what things were gain to me, these I have counted loss for Christ. Yet indeed I also count all things loss for the excellence of the knowledge of Christ Jesus my Lord, for whom I have suffered the loss of all things, and count them as rubbish, that I may gain Christ and be found in Him, not having my own righteousness, which is from the law, but that which is through faith in Christ, the righteousness which is from God by faith...Not that I have already attained, or am already perfected; but I press on, that I may lay hold of that for which Christ Jesus has also laid hold of me. Brethren, I do not count myself to have apprehended; but one thing I do, forgetting those things which are behind and reaching forward to those things which are ahead, I press toward the goal for the prize of the upward call of God in Christ Jesus (Philippians 3:7–9, 12–14).

Like Paul, forget the past and look ahead to an exciting future when your dream will come to pass. God loves wild people and their wild dreams, including yours. Don't let your dream die and don't take it with you to the grave. Walk with God as one of His wild men and let Him bring your dream to reality.

PERSONAL DREAM JOURNAL

CHAPTER SEVEN

Messed-Up Christians

Today as in the days of the Bible, God loves wild people and He loves to use wild people.

As I was writing for my first CD, *Honey in the Rock*, the Lord spoke something to me that changed my life forever. He said, "Jimmie, everyone is messed up, *including you.*" That may not sound very profound to you, but it changed my life. You see, I was a Christian who thought everyone was messed up *except* me. I was in the business of casting the first stone because I believed that everyone else had problems, but not me. Of course, I was deceived because all of us fall short of God's glory. All of us miss the mark (see Romans 3:23). There is only one who is right and His name is Jesus.

Don't Take Your Dreams to the Grave

Gaining this new understanding changed the way I looked at people. The more I acknowledged my own flaws, the more compassion I was able to show for everyone else because I knew I needed them to have compassion on me also. I was able to accept the fact that *all* of us have problems. All of us fail every day in one way or another; all of us except Jesus. The Bible says that we are in the process of being transformed into the image of Christ. Day by day we are learning, growing, and coming to a greater understanding and application of truth in our lives—truth that will lead us more and more into victory and success.

Realizing how messed up I was helped me understand that *it's okay not to be perfect.* God sees all our mistakes, loves us anyway, and is still willing to work with us as we make our way through them. In the wake of this new understanding I wrote the song "Doctor, Doctor" as a confession of my own condition and the acknowledgement of my need for Jesus to help me—the need for Jesus to help all of us:

Doctor, Doctor, can I have a talk with you?

Doctor, Doctor, can I have a talk with you?

I need a Great Physician.

Got a soul condition...

You see, I had to change the way I looked at people. I had to start being part of mankind instead of living in some kind of euphoric world that religion had created for me. I had to tear down the "us" and "them" mentality: "us" (the saved) vs. "them" (the sinners). Jesus never thought that way or He never would have associated with the kind of people He did. As long as we have this kind of thinking we will never be able to reach our world with the gospel. Have you ever noticed how many Christians go around acting like they have all the answers? I used to, but not anymore. (At least, I try not to!) Maybe you're one of them. If so, lighten up. You don't have all the answers and you know it. Since everybody else thinks they do, too, they won't believe you if you act that way, so what's the point?

This know-it-all mentality and acting like we're perfect when really we're messed up are two of the reasons why the world has so much contempt for the church. If we have all the answers, then why are Christians failing just like the world? Why are there as many divorces in the church as there are outside the church? Why are our kids just as messed up as the kids of our unsaved neighbors? We've got to stop play-acting and be honest about ourselves and our problems.

Jesus alone has all the answers. It is up to each individual to personally discover the answers for him- or herself, and the only place to find those answers is in Jesus. Our message must be that *Jesus is the answer.*

Changing Our Image

We all may be messed up, but Jesus is not. So we need to work to change our image, to acknowledge our weaknesses and failings. That way, when the world looks at us and hears our words they won't encounter a contradiction. Instead of seeing us trying to hide or deny our weaknesses, they will see Christ *in* us and how He has transformed us through and in spite of our weaknesses.

First John 2:2 says, "And He Himself is the propitiation for our sins, and not for ours only but also for the whole world." In this verse, "the whole world" includes us—the followers of Jesus. He is the "propitiation," or the "mercy seat" for our sins. Jesus didn't view the world as "us" and "them." He viewed the world as the whole of mankind.

We must also adopt an inclusive view of people before the gospel will really become effective in our world. Too often we tend to be very exclusive. We're very picky about who we accept and who we will associate with. If we approach our world with this kind of exclusive mentality we will be rejected, and rightly so, because we will come across to them as thinking we are better than they are.

We must be inclusive in our attitude toward people without accepting or condoning their sin. If we love them with the love of Jesus, in time *He* will deal with the sin problem, not us.

We must be inclusive in our attitude toward people without accepting or condoning their sin.

In relation to this, there is a story I like to tell that happened to me in church. There was a couple who were receiving help from our church and eventually they expressed interest in joining the church as members. The mother of one of them came to me to ask if the church would accept them as members and said, "They're not married. They're living in sin. Will the church still accept them?"

And I replied, "I don't remember Jesus rejecting anyone because of sin; in fact that is the very reason why He came. So, we will accept them as *members*, but *not* as a *couple*. They will either embrace the truth of Christ or they will run from it." Sure enough, six months later, one of them came seeking help. Here's the clincher: this couple was homosexual.

Inclusiveness does not mean accepting or tolerating or compromising with sin. It does mean that we allow the Holy Spirit time to convict each person of his or her own sin. This is not our job but the Holy Spirit's. It does mean that we don't reject anybody whom Christ died for, and He died for everybody. That's pretty inclusive!

So how do we change our image? We change it by modeling something else. In everything that God does to teach us, He first models it for us. Genesis 1:29 says that God gave "every herb that yields seed" and "every tree whose fruit yields seed." In Genesis 2:8, God "planted a garden" in Eden. We don't know if man was there when God planted the garden, but every other time that God was on the earth, man was with Him. I assume that God was modeling, teaching the man what to do with his seed.

The same is true with Jesus. He came not only to die for our sins but also to show us what God is like and to model for us what a new-creation man was like.

Here's my point: if we are going to change the culture as believers we must *model* to the world the reality of the New Testament, new-creation inclusive life. We must demonstrate the realities of the love of God for all people: the down-and-outers as well as the up-and-outers.

Working with Messed-Up Christians

I have had the honor to be around some pastors who have fallen into sin. That's right; I said, *"honor."* When I mentioned this to some of my other ministry friends they warned me to be careful about my association with these men who had fallen. Needless to say, in the light of my own new understanding, I had a few choice words to say to those fellows! If we are going to be wild in showing the love of God, then we are going to have to start first with ourselves: those inside of the household of faith who have fallen.

I consider it an honor to extend love and help to those who have fallen. When I first met one of these men he said to me, "I guess you heard about how I messed on myself." I said yes. Then he asked, "What do you think?"

"Did Jesus forgive you?" I asked in return.

"Yes," he replied.

"Did your wife forgive you?"

"Yes."

"Well then," I said, "I guess it really isn't any of my business, is it?"

Sad to say, my response to him was completely different from the way this man of God had been treated by many. He had been humiliated and humbled by his sin, and even though he confessed it and was reconciled with his family, he saw very little of Jesus in the attitude and response he received from others in the Lord. Why do we find it so easy to forget the plain instructions of Galatians 6:1–2?

> *Brethren, if a man is overtaken in any trespass, you who are spiritual restore such a one in a spirit of gentleness, considering yourself lest you also be tempted. Bear one another's burdens, and so fulfill the law of Christ.*

Think of Jesus' example with Simon Peter. On the night before Jesus was crucified, Peter denied Him three times. After His resurrection, Jesus came to Peter on the beach and three times gently loved the disheartened, humbled fisherman back into a healed relationship (see John 21:15–19).

Like Jesus, I want to be a peacemaker and a restorer, one who holds people up rather than tears them down. That's what Jesus modeled, and that's the way He wants us to be.

God Is Not Mad at You

God is wild in that He will go to the end with somebody in order to redeem them. One of the board members of my ministry is Dr. Jim Richards, a great pastor and gifted writer. When I first got around Jim I didn't know what to think about some of his teaching. The first time I heard him say, "God is not mad at you," it freaked out my little Christian brain.

God is not mad at us? Then what about this verse: "God *is* a just judge, and God is angry *with the wicked* every day" (Psalm 7:11)? That is a true passage of Scripture from the Old Covenant. The Bible teaches us that we have a New Covenant in Christ, a better covenant based on better promises (see Hebrews 8:6). When Jesus died on the cross, His death satisfied God's divine justice and judgment on our sins, and not ours only, but also the sins of the whole world. His resurrection guaranteed a new life, eternal life, for all who would believe on Him by faith. God poured out all His judgment, anger, and wrath against sin upon Jesus on the cross. And so we entered into a new time with God, a time of God's grace extended over our planet rather than judgment. Please don't misunderstand me; God is a God of judgment and a time is coming when God will judge us all. But that time is not now. God is not looking down at you from Heaven just waiting for you to make a mistake so He can "zap" you for your sin. No, God is looking at you in order for you to give Him the opportunity to forgive you.

Jesus came as the Prince of Peace preaching the gospel of peace. God is not mad at you. God loves you. He sees you as you are (sin and everything) and wants to forgive you. Now *that* is wild! That is love to the extreme; *crazy* love; *wild love*. It is a love that compels me to love in return. Doesn't the love that God has for you make you want to give your life to Jesus and follow Him forever? Go on and live the *wild love life* that God has prepared for you. Dream your dreams. Then get ready to move because God wants to move you into your *dream season*!

CHAPTER EIGHT

Dream Season

How well I remember the day the Lord spoke a word to me that profoundly changed my life. I was 24 years old, Sherri, the kids, and I were attending a camp-meeting. I'm not talking about those modern sissy camp-meetings that you see advertised in magazines that are inside a nice air-conditioned church and where you stay in hotels. This was a *real* camp-meeting. I mean we slept in tents, and cooked our food over an open campfire, really roughing it.

The meetings themselves were held in a little makeshift amphitheater with a stage that consisted of little more than a few pieces of plywood nailed onto some timbers. Some overhanging trees provided a little bit of shade for the speakers.

Don't Take Your Dreams to the Grave

I really loved going to those meetings. Why? I guess it's because I was hungry for God and out there in the woods was a wild place to be. After all, the Lord is certainly no stranger to wild and natural places. God spoke to Moses from a burning bush on a mountain in the wilderness and led and fed the children of Israel for 40 years in the wilderness. David got to know God in the wilderness, sitting on the hillsides day after day and night after night tending his family's sheep. Jesus was tempted in the wilderness and regularly during His earthly ministry rose early in the morning and went out to the "lonely" places to pray. Yes, the wilderness is a great place to meet God.

One day during this camp-meeting an older lady named Lucille Kline was scheduled to minister. Earlier in the day I had briefly met both her and her husband. I found out later that both of these ministers had spent time ministering to my great-grandfather. Now they were ready to minister to me.

Sister Kline took to the platform and began to minister a message that has stuck with me ever since. You really know that something is from God when God speaks to you and you hear it with your life and not with just your ears. It echoes into the very fabric of who you are and is not some passing moment, there and then gone.

Opening her Bible to the Book of Job, Sister Kline read the words that have reverberated in my spirit for the last 25 years:

> *For God may speak in one way, or in another, yet man does not perceive it. In a dream, in a vision of the night, when deep sleep falls upon men, while slumbering on their beds, then He opens the ears of men, and seals their instruction* (Job 33:14–16).

One of the first truths about God that is revealed in the Scriptures is that God is a talking God.

These words impressed two things on my heart that day: the truth that God speaks and that He would speak to me through dreams and visions.

One of the first truths about God that is revealed in the Scriptures is that God is a talking God. He speaks and His voice has the power to create, power to change, power to comfort, power to judge, power to encourage, and power to do anything else He desires.

Those verses from Job that Sister Kline read also taught me that God is not limited in His means or His methods of communicating with me. If He has to, He will speak "in one way, or in another." The moment I heard those words at that primitive camp-meeting I knew immediately that I could rest in the comfort of the Scriptures that God was speaking and that I was going to hear Him! He would make sure of it.

I knew that if I could just get that transaction working in my life that I would be okay and that I would experience victory. The method God uses to speak to us isn't as important as the fact that He does speak and that we hear Him. Hearing God is the important thing.

Sometimes it can be hard to hear God while we're awake, especially in the busy and hectic crunch of life that so many of us live every day. That is one reason why God often chooses to speak to us at night in our dreams. God speaks "in a dream, in a vision of the night, when deep sleep falls upon men, while slumbering on their beds." That's when God "opens the ears of men, and seals their instruction."

What a relief it was to me to realize that even if I was unable to hear God while I was awake, He was able to speak to me even when I was asleep! That understanding of God's faithfulness and ability in speaking to me created a stronghold of faith and confidence that I still rely on today.

God Speaks through Dreams

Knowing that I could hear God changed everything, especially knowing that He would invade my dreams. What a fantastic thought! Dreams are fuel for life and a common way that God communicated in the New Testament. In the Gospel of Matthew, God speaks to Joseph in a dream to assure him that the baby that his fiancée, Mary, is carrying was conceived by the Holy Spirit and is the promised Messiah. Later in another dream, the Lord warns Joseph to flee to Egypt with Mary and the child Jesus to escape the murderous wrath of Herod. Even the wise men receive a dream from God warning them not to return to Herod as he has requested. After Herod's death, God tells Joseph in another dream that it is safe to return home.

In the Book of Acts, Saul (soon to be Paul) sees a vision of Christ while on the road to Damascus to persecute Christians. A few days later, a Damascan Christian named Ananias receives a vision from God telling him to lay hands on Saul and restore his sight. In another chapter Cornelius, a God-fearing Roman centurion, has a vision while praying in which the Lord tells him to send for Simon Peter. Meanwhile, Peter himself has a vision from God that prepares him to go to Cornelius' home without any hesitation, even though devout Jews would not defile themselves by entering the home of a Gentile.

God readily spoke to His people through dreams and visions in the New Testament, and He is just as interested in communicating to you and me through our dreams today. Look at the promise from the Book of Joel that Peter spoke on the Day of Pentecost, the very day that promise was fulfilled:

> *But this is what was spoken by the prophet Joel: And it shall come to pass in the last days, says God, that I will pour out of My Spirit on all flesh; your sons and your daughters shall prophesy, your young men shall see visions, your old men shall dream dreams. And on My menservants and on My maidservants I will pour out My Spirit in those days; and they shall prophesy* (Acts 2:16–18, quoting Joel 2:28–29).

Now don't freak out just because it says, "old men shall dream dreams." You don't have to be old for God to use a dream to speak to you. The verse also says that "young men shall see visions," which is close to the same thing. Joseph in the Old Testament was just a boy when he started having dreams from God.

The point is that God will communicate with us through our dreams. Physicians tell us that we all dream every night even though most of us don't remember our dreams. If God speaks to us in a dream it's because He has something to say to us, and He will make sure not only that we remember it but also that we understand it and that we know it was Him who spoke to us. Dreams are a powerful and meaningful way to hear from God.

Throughout history dreams have inspired ordinary men and women to achieve extraordinary things and to press on to victory in spite of incredible obstacles.

Dreams Are the Desires of Our Heart

But I want us also to look at dreams from a different angle: as referring to the strongest and deepest desires of our heart. Those desires—dreams that have always been inside us even before we were aware of them—can be some of the most powerful motivators in our lives. Some people call those desires destiny. Call them whatever you like, but those dreams of ours also contain some of the most important divine information we have. God plants dreams in our hearts, and those dreams are clues to our potential and to the specific destiny that He desires for each of us.

Throughout history dreams have inspired ordinary men and women to achieve extraordinary things and to press on to victory in spite of incredible obstacles. It was a dream of freedom for Scotland that inspired William "Braveheart" Wallace to rally an army and defy the might of England. It was a dream of controlled, powered flight that inspired two bicycle mechanics from Dayton, Ohio, Wilbur and Orville Wright, to design, build, and fly the world's first successful engine-powered airplane. It was a dream of healthy children that inspired Dr. Jonas Salk to develop a vaccine against polio, so that no more people would be confined to life in an iron lung. Such examples are virtually endless.

Dreams may be one of the strongest motivators in our lives, but they can also be suppressed to the point where they are almost forgotten under the pressures of life. Whatever it is that is stopping you from living your dream, perhaps the time has come to resurrect that dream and start pursuing it.

Don't think that you don't have a dream. You do. Everybody does. So what is your dream? Do you dream of raising great kids or having a great marriage or enjoying a rewarding career or even all three? Do you dream of making a difference in the lives of people? Do you dream of being a musician or a writer or an artist? Whatever your dream may be, my question to you is, what are you doing about it? Are you living your dream? Are you pursuing your dream? Or are you still waiting for the "right moment" to get started?

I found in my own experience that just having a dream isn't enough; you have to be prepared to follow after and live that dream. Desire alone won't do the trick. In my travels I meet many people with suppressed dreams, people who put their dreams on hold for a variety of reasons. Now they believe they will never realize their dreams because they are too old. Too much time has gone by and they assume the opportunity has come and gone. They're wrong.

It's never too late to pursue your dream. As long as you are alive and breathing you have the chance to pursue what you were meant to do. Age is no factor. Moses was 80 before he came into his destiny as the deliverer of Israel. Abraham was 100 years old when his son Isaac was born, the child of promise through whom Abraham would become the father of a nation.

Don't Take Your Dreams to the Grave

Time is no factor either. The important thing to remember about dreams is that they sometimes take time in order to come to pass, but if God has planted the dream and you pursue it in faith and patience, it will come to pass in God's good time. Abraham waited 25 years between the promise of Isaac and the fulfillment. Joseph was only a teenager when he first had dreams regarding his destiny, but more than 20 years passed before those dreams came true. He had to wait a long time for his dream season—*but it came.*

And yours will too!

CHAPTER NINE

From Dream to Destiny

Joseph is the most famous dreamer in the Bible. Even as a young man his dreams affected and directed his life. Because he was his father's favorite, Joseph was resented by his half-brothers. Their jealousy was so strong, in fact, that the Bible says that they couldn't speak a civil word to him. Then one day Joseph made it worse by telling his brothers about a dream he had:

> *So he said to them, "Please hear this dream which I have dreamed: There we were, binding sheaves in the field. Then behold, my sheaf arose and also stood upright; and indeed your sheaves stood all around and bowed down to my sheaf." And his brothers*

101

said to him, "Shall you indeed reign over us? Or shall you indeed have dominion over us?" So they hated him even more for his dreams and for his words (Genesis 37:6–8).

Not long after, Joseph had another dream:

Then he dreamed still another dream and told it to his brothers, and said, "Look, I have dreamed another dream. And this time, the sun, the moon, and the eleven stars bowed down to me." So he told it to his father and his brothers; and his father rebuked him and said to him, "What is this dream that you have dreamed? Shall your mother and I and your brothers indeed come to bow down to the earth before you?" And his brothers envied him, but his father kept the matter in mind (Genesis 37:9–11).

At 17, Joseph probably understood very little of what his dreams meant, but he apparently thought they were important. Many years would pass before Joseph saw his dreams fulfilled, but God used those experiences to train and mature and prepare him for his destiny. In the end, Joseph's years of waiting and maturing were a small price to pay for the dream that was fulfilled in his life.

Sold into slavery by his jealous brothers, Joseph wound up in the home of Potiphar, captain of the guard for the pharaoh, where he soon demonstrated his character and administrative skills and became overseer of his master's house. Falsely accused by his master's wife of trying to seduce her, Joseph landed in prison where his skills again served him well when the prison warden put him in charge of all the other prisoners.

While in prison, Joseph had the opportunity to interpret the dreams of two of Pharaoh's servants, his butler and his baker. Both dreams came true just as Joseph had said. A couple of years later, Pharaoh himself had two troubling dreams that he could not understand. When none of Pharaoh's advisers could interpret the dreams, the butler remembered Joseph.

When brought before Pharaoh, Joseph correctly interpreted his dreams as predicting seven years of plenty followed by seven years of famine. Joseph also recommended that Pharaoh appoint an overseer to manage affairs during the seven good years to store up resources against the seven years of famine. The pharaoh, recognizing Joseph's character and skills, immediately appointed him to the position.

Don't Take Your Dreams to the Grave

This was Joseph's moment, the moment for which God had been preparing him all this time. Joseph became prime minister, second only to Pharaoh, and was instrumental in saving the people of Egypt from starvation, and his own family as well. Eventually, Joseph's brothers came to Egypt to buy food and, in fulfillment of Joseph's dreams so many years before, bowed before Joseph, although they did not recognize him.

Joseph's destiny was to save Egypt and his own family and set the stage for the ancestors of Israel to migrate to Egypt where they would grow into a mighty nation. A powerful dream and an awesome destiny, but it took many years to come to pass. But when the time was right, Joseph was ready and God made it happen.

I think it is interesting to note that Joseph's dreams didn't start to come to pass until he became interested and involved in other people's dreams: first of the butler and baker and later of Pharaoh himself. Like Joseph, we may find ourselves in a "dream season" when our own dreams seem to be elusive or on hold, and we wonder if they will ever come true. If we trust God, they will come true in His time. Meanwhile, Joseph's story can teach us so much about dealing with our own "dream season."

Involve Yourself in the Dreams of Others

First of all, we can't become so focused on our own dreams that we don't involve ourselves in the dreams of others. The Christian life is a life of service and giving. We cannot grow into the people of destiny God wants us to be if we focus exclusively on our own self-interests. It is of the utmost importance that you find another dreamer whom you can serve. This is critical in the fulfillment of your own dreams. Jesus said it like this: "And if you have not been faithful in what is another man's, who will give you what is your own?" (Luke 16:12). In order to start the process of fulfilling your dream, you must find someone whom you can help to fulfill his or her dreams and give your whole heart's service to them.

It is of the utmost importance that you find another dreamer whom you can serve.

I spent 23 years serving other men's dreams. That may seem like a long time to you; I know it did to me. But I also know that time is something I don't control and I needed all of that time for God to prepare me to walk in the fulfillment of my own dreams. Because of that, I don't regret a day of those 23 years. They were all very necessary, both for me and for the men I served. If I had ventured out any sooner, I probably would have failed because the time was not right.

God Controls the Time of Fulfillment

That brings us to another point from Joseph's story: God controls the time of fulfillment. Psalm 31: 14–15a says, "But as for me, I trust in You, O LORD; I say, You *are* my God. My times *are* in Your hand."

Once I was ministering in France and a pastor gave me a plaque inscribed with the words of Psalm 31:15 in French. The French word for "times" is *destines*. In other words, our destinies are in the hand of the Lord, not in our hands. God would not release Joseph into his destiny until the time was right. Timing is everything. It's not enough just to have a dream. Our dream has a time attached to it for its fulfillment and if we don't trust the Lord to fulfill it in His time, we could miss altogether what God wants to do through us. Joseph may have expected his dream to come to pass right away. As we have seen, it took more than 20 years, but when God's time came, Joseph's dream came to pass in a hurry. Just think, Joseph spent 20 years becoming an overnight success!

You Have What It Takes to See Your Dream Come to Pass

A good pastor friend of mine, Gene Saunders, taught me that disappointment is a demon spirit. In fact, I believe now that everything with the prefix "dis-" in it is probably from the devil: discouragement, disunity, dissatisfaction, disease, disharmony, etc. Inevitably, disappointment will lie along the route to your dream fulfillment. There will be times when you think you're going to make it only to see it elude you once again.

Disappointment is a real force that will attempt to persuade you to look at things other than the dream; to focus on thoughts and aspects that will turn you aside from pursuing your destiny. But God gave you your dream to keep in front of you—to be your vision—so that you can have a reference point against disappointment. If you can *see* your dream, you can *do* it. It may take awhile, but don't let disappointment keep you from pressing on.

When God creates a dream in our heart He sees the end from the beginning and knows as the giver of the dream that the recipient of the dream is qualified to see that it comes to pass. In other words, when God plants a dream in your heart, He also places in you everything you need to bring it to pass. He wants you to succeed! God wants you to fulfill your dream! God never does anything without a purpose. He would not have given you your dream if He didn't want you to fulfill it and didn't believe that you could.

Surround yourself with people who believe in you and your dream.

The main threat to fulfilling your dream is doubt and unbelief. Unbelief can paralyze you and effectively destroy the dream God has given. Therefore, you must protect yourself against doubt and unbelief. How?

Encourage yourself in the Lord. David came home from battle to find his town burned and his family kidnapped. His men were turning on him when the Bible says something amazing: "David encouraged himself in the Lord his God" (1 Samuel 30:6 KJV). If you are going to hold on to your dream you must learn how to encourage yourself in the Lord. Personally, I'm the type of guy that requires a constant stream of encouragement; no, not a stream but a river; no, not a river but an ocean!

Surround yourself with people who believe in you. Bob Ingle, one of my board members, called me on the first day that I started Ransom Ministries and asked what he could do for me. Feeling insecure in my new ministry adventure, I said, "Call me on Monday and tell me I did the right thing." Every Monday for the past several years Bob has called me and said, "You did the right thing." Even today, years later, I still look forward to that call because I need constant encouragement. Surround yourself with people who believe in you and your dream.

Never let go of your dream—no matter how long it takes to come to pass. Time can prove to be one of your greatest assets. Most of us dislike the patience factor but it is patience that will mature your dream like nothing else will. In the New Testament, the Greek word for "patience" is *hupomone*, which means "cheerful constancy or to say the same thing." Time will prove whether you hang on the dream or say something different. So by all means, keep talking about your dream and keep saying the same thing.

Your dream is worth hanging on to. It has great value and if you find yourself in the season where it is not coming to pass, hang on and don't let go because soon enough you will enter your dream season. And when God's time comes, get ready, because He will take you to the crossroads.

PERSONAL DREAM JOURNAL

_____
_____
_____
_____
_____
_____
_____
_____
_____
_____
_____
_____
_____
_____
_____
_____
_____
_____
_____
_____
_____
_____

CHAPTER TEN

Going to "The Crossroads"

It was warm that May morning in 2003 as I packed up my Harley and "headed south out of Memphis on Highway 61." (That's a quote from my song "Take it Back".) Accompanied by Brian Zahnd, a pastor and friend of mine, our plan was to ride the Mississippi Delta from Memphis to Natchez and visit all the historic blues sites. If you know me, you would probably expect that this trip was my idea. Well, it wasn't; it was Brian's.

Nevertheless, I was eager to go. During my teen years I often spent my summers on the streets in Memphis doing drugs and playing the music. I have great memories of Memphis in May and this motorcycle trip would prove to be a memorable one as well.

Don't Take Your Dreams to the Grave

There is nothing really scenic about Highway 61 and the Mississippi Delta. Highway 61 is just a flat road and the scenery is the same: flat river delta land punctuated by farms and the occasional delta town. Yet this part of the United States holds a mystique and wields an influence in our history far beyond its outward appearance. The Delta's influence in music history in particular is huge. Almost all of the founders of blues music—which is, of course, the root of rock and roll and a whole bunch of other music genres—came from this Delta. Over the years I suppose thousands or even tens of thousands of pilgrims have made a trip similar to ours.

As we rode down the highway my mind buzzed with thoughts of all the blues greats, both past and present, who have traveled this same road. Our first stop was to be Clarksdale, Mississippi, the home of blues greats like Muddy Waters, John Lee Hooker, Robert Johnson, and others. Brian and I didn't really have a solid plan as to where we were going. We were just travelin' south. Sounds like fun, doesn't it? Let me tell you, it was!

As we entered Clarksdale we pulled up to an intersection and stopped. It looked just like thousands of other intersections in thousands of other small towns everywhere. That is, until I saw the sign that said, "JCT HWY 61 & 49." This was the spot! A glance to my left confirmed it. There it was: the sign marking this place as "The Crossroads." According to blues historians, The Crossroads is where several of the most mysterious transactions in blues history are said to have taken place.

I already knew that people from all over the world come to this very place for a couple of reasons. They want to see for themselves the very spot where Robert Johnson and several other blues musicians supposedly sold their souls to the devil and many hope to have a similar transaction also! No one knows for sure if this is the actual spot, but many people believe that it was right here where Robert Johnson made his infamous transaction with the devil.

Robert Johnson was a marginal guitarist who suddenly became an outstanding guitarist seemly overnight. He also became one of the most influential musicians of the last century, leaving his mark on the music of such artists as The Rolling Stones, Eric Clapton, and Keb Mo, to name only a few. When people asked Robert how he became such a great guitar player he would tell the story of how he sold his soul to the devil at The Crossroads.

As wild as this tale may sound, people from all over the world come to the Mississippi Delta and

Clarksdale looking to have a similar experience. Now here I was in May 2003 sitting at The Crossroads. I, however, was not looking for an experience with the devil, but as always, I was expecting the favor of God.

Meeting Doc

We pulled through the intersection and off the road to find a map of historic blues sites. Suddenly, a mysterious man in a pickup appeared. It seemed as though he came out of nowhere. He pulled up next to our bikes, poked his head out the window, and said in a gruff, stern voice, "Are you boys here to look at my town"?

"Yes," I responded. "What should we see?"

As we chatted some more the conversation came around to food, especially barbecue. You can't really have the blues without good barbecue.

Brian asked the stranger where we could find some. The man pointed and said, "Right there, at Abe's at The Crossroads. Come on, I'll take you over there. By the way, my name is Doc."

As we sat and ate, Doc asked about our vocations. Pointing to Brian I responded, "This guy is a pastor and I am an evangelist but also a blues guitarist." Doc said, "Blues? Have you got CDs and stuff?"

"Yes I do."

"Well," Doc continued, "I know people here in Clarksdale who are into the blues. Did you know that Morgan Freeman, the actor, has a club downtown? Come on, I'll introduce you to him." So off we went on this first adventure since arriving at The Crossroads.

Any day, no matter how normal it seems, can be instantly transformed by a simple yet profound defining moment.

As it turned out, Morgan Freeman wasn't at his club, Ground Zero, that day, but Doc introduced us to several other people in the blues community in Clarksdale.

A Defining Moment

When I got home later that week I sent Doc a thank you card. I was thrilled and amazed by the entire experience. Somehow I knew that God was behind our encounter with Doc and the people he introduced us to. That's one of the many things I like about following Jesus; you never know where the road is going to take you. Any day, no matter how normal it seems, can be instantly transformed by a simple yet profound defining moment. Everything may seem mundane yet suddenly change dramatically.

About 90 days after my trip I got an email from Doc requesting my phone number. Doc called and said, "I have just been made the co-chairman of the first ever blues festival to be held at The Crossroads and I want you and your band to be the first band that we book." Well, I was off the chart with excitement! Just imagine, *me* playing in Clarksdale, Mississippi, at "The Crossroads Blues Festival!"

My band did, indeed, play the festival. In March 2004 we also played at Morgan Freeman's club, Ground Zero, in downtown Clarksdale. The place was packed with bikers drinking beer. In my song "Love Running" I scream the third verse, "Jesus, will you take me as I am?" I wondered how the crowd that day would respond. Then the time came and I just let it rip, and to my amazement, a roar of applause and cheers came from the crowd at the name of Jesus. You see, when people hear the gospel they love it. This day at Ground Zero has become one of the most outstanding defining moments of my ministry, and all because I was at the right place at the right time.

"Showin' Up"

People ask me all the time what kind of ministry I have and I always say, "I have the ministry of *showin' up*!" That may sound simple but I have discovered that it is the key, for me at least, to opening up the vast treasure chest of God's favor.

After over 20 years of following Jesus I finally came to the understanding (why did it take so long?) that Christ is *in* me! Paul says in Galatians, "I have been crucified with Christ; it is no longer I who live, but *Christ lives in me*; and the life which I now live in the flesh I live by faith in the Son of God, who loved me and gave Himself for me" (Galatians 2:20 emphasis added). I had known that Scripture for years, but it had just never become real to me.

But the moment I finally understood that Jesus really *was* in me, it completely transformed my thinking. I am no longer on a quest to "find God." I am on a quest to discover the fullness of the riches of Jesus who happens to live in me. So in my ministry of "showin' up," when I show up somewhere, I expect Jesus to show up there also because He came with me. Whether I'm preaching in church on a Sunday morning or playing the blues at a festival somewhere, I know and expect Jesus to be there with me and to work through me.

That day at The Crossroads I just showed up and Jesus took over, ordering my steps and making divine connections in a very natural, yet supernatural way. I guess you could say that the supernatural is when the natural becomes super! The day we played at Morgan Freeman's club, Ground Zero, was a divine moment for me, for Sherri, and for the band as well as for all those who came to hear us play.

When we arrived at Ground Zero to set up, the sound man came out and introduced himself. "Hi. My name is Wolff." He was a bearded, tattooed young man in his 20s and he and I became quick friends. Wolff helped us load in and setup. Before. I left the club I gave him a copy of my DVD, *LIVE on the 4ᵗʰ of July.*

A few days later I received an email from Wolff complimenting me on the quality of our performance and commenting on the quality of the interaction he saw between the band members both on and off the stage. He also told me that he had watched the DVD and specifically my testimony, the track titled "As the Story Goes." Then he wrote, "You have given hope to my shattered faith. I have been through some stuff." I was thrilled to read Wolff's words, for I knew they meant that he was making a new commitment to Jesus, which I later confirmed was, indeed, the case.

At another time I also learned that, as a result of our encounter at The Crossroads and our playing the blues festival there, that Doc also rededicated his life to Christ. God is so good. That moment at The Crossroads did so much to encourage and motivate me to believe for more of the favor of God.

I believe that God has a "crossroads" experience for you, too; perhaps many of them.

I believe that God has a "crossroads" experience for you, too; perhaps many of them. Just keep walking in faith and keep "showin' up" and He will work in and through you. And one of these days you will find yourself walking toward, and then into, your dream.

Personal Dream Journal

CHAPTER ELEVEN

Walking by Faith

In the right time and place God will bring you into your dream. The right place? Where is that place? The right time? When is the right time and how do you know? These are the kinds of questions that people with delayed or deferred or suppressed dreams often ask. "If there's a 'right time' for my dream, how will I know when that time has arrived? If there's a 'right place' for my dream, how will I know when I get there?"

Part of the answer lies in remembering that time is in God's hands. He has a dream for you just like He does for me, but your dream will be different from mine. In God's plan there is a right place and a right time—a "crossroads"—for your dream to come to pass. The best thing you can do is to walk by faith and trust God to show you when your season has come. It says in Proverbs:

Trust in the Lord with all your heart, and lean not on your own understanding; in all your ways acknowledge Him, and He shall direct your paths (Proverbs 3:5–6).

To trust means to place your full and complete confidence in someone or something. Trust with complete confidence that the God who planted your dream in your heart will also lead you into the season of its fulfillment.

God never does anything halfway. Whatever God initiates, He completes. The apostle Paul stated it this way: "He who has begun a good work in you will complete it until the day of Jesus Christ" (Philippians 1:6b). In context, Paul was talking specifically about the work of salvation that God effects in the life of every believer, but the same holds true for anything God initiates in our lives. In other words, whatever God has started to do in your life,

Only you can prevent the fulfillment of the dream God gave you.

including the dreams and desires that He planted in your heart, He will bring to pass just as He has always intended.

The key is to walk by faith. Only you can prevent the fulfillment of the dream God gave you. If you don't believe that your dream can come true or that God can bring it to pass or that He wants to, you can go through your entire life frustrated and never fulfill your destiny. God gave you a dream but He won't force it on you. You must believe, walk by faith, and be willing to submit yourself to His will and to "in all your ways acknowledge Him." You must allow Him in His time and place to bring you into your season of dream fulfillment.

Psalm 37:4–5 says:

Delight yourself also in the Lord, and He shall give you the desires of your heart. Commit your way to the Lord, trust also in Him, and He shall bring it to pass.

This promise is for everyone who has come to faith in Jesus—without exception. Our past doesn't matter. It makes no difference whether or not we think we deserve it. Our right to claim this promise has nothing to do with our feelings or with our deeds, whether good or bad. Jesus qualifies us for the promise. Commit your way to the Lord and let Him take care of everything else, including your dreams. He will bring to pass all that He desires for you. He will let you know when your season has come and He will orchestrate your circumstances so that you are in the right time and place.

The Favor of the Lord

Job 10:12 says, "You have granted me life and favor, and Your care has preserved my spirit." Favor is an attribute of God that means to afford advantages for success. In other words, when you have God's favor He gives you advantages that help you succeed even in spite of obstacles in your path. No matter what else is going on around you, everything in your life just seems to flow more smoothly and to work better. Things that seem like they shouldn't work out, do anyway; difficulties that seem insurmountable are overcome more easily than you imagined.

I have known and enjoyed the favor of the Lord on my life even in extremely difficult times. In fact, often it is easier to see God's favor best during those times of lack and trouble when it seems that only He can bring us through. But I have also come to recognize God's favor in times of success, and of the two, I like the latter the best.

When we come to the understanding that we are in Christ and that Christ is in us, some of the attributes of God, like His favor, just flow out of our experience. Sure, it takes faith. We must hear and do the Word of God, but once that is established in our lives, we can expect the flow of God's favor to be an abiding reality.

Maybe in your life and experience right now you have trouble believing that God's favor is upon you. Let me assure you: if you believe in Jesus, God's favor is upon you. He loves you and wants to see your dreams come to pass. If you still have trouble truly believing that God loves you and that His favor and blessings are inclined toward you, consider these Scriptures:

The Lord has appeared of old to me, saying: "Yes, I have loved you with an everlasting love; therefore with lovingkindness I have drawn you (Jeremiah 31:3).

For I know the thoughts that I think toward you, says the Lord, thoughts of peace and not of evil, to give you a future and a hope. Then you will call upon Me and go and pray to Me, and I will listen to you. And you will seek Me and find Me, when you search for Me with all your heart (Jeremiah 29:11–13).

Though the Lord is on high, yet He regards the lowly; but the proud He knows from afar (Psalm 138:6).

For You, O Lord, will bless the righteous; with favor You will surround him as with a shield (Psalm 5:12).

For whoever finds me [wisdom, as a personification of God's Word] *finds life, and obtains favor from the Lord* (Proverbs 8:35).

A good man obtains favor from the Lord, but a man of wicked intentions He will condemn (Proverbs 12:2).

For the eyes of the Lord run to and fro throughout the whole earth, to show Himself strong on behalf of those whose heart is loyal to Him (2 Chronicles 16:9a).

The eyes of the Lord are on the righteous, and His ears are open to their cry....The righteous cry out, and the Lord hears, and delivers them out of all their troubles. The Lord is near to those who have a broken heart, and saves such as have a contrite spirit (Psalm 34:15, 17–18).

But God demonstrates His own love toward us, in that while we were still sinners, Christ died for us (Romans 5:8).

What then shall we say to these things? If God is for us, who can be against us? He who did not spare His own Son, but delivered Him up for us all, how shall He not with Him also freely give us all things? (Romans 8:31–32)

For I am persuaded that neither death nor life, nor angels nor principalities nor powers, nor things present nor things to come, nor height nor depth, nor any other created thing, shall be able to separate us from the love of God which is in Christ Jesus our Lord (Romans 8:38–39).

These, of course, are only a few of the many Scriptures that affirm that God loves us and that His favor rests upon us. As you walk in faith with God's favor upon you, your success is assured as you let Him guide your paths. At the right time and in the right place He will help you fulfill your dream and bring you into your destiny.

When you show up in life you can expect not only the favor of God but also His presence to be with you even in the darkest places. Think about it: you know Jesus lives in you, so He goes with you everywhere you go. And when you show up He is there with you looking for an opportunity "to afford advantages for your success."

All Things Work Together for Good

When we know that we are in Christ and He is in us, life becomes much more than just a search for meaning and purpose or a chase after one spiritual experience after another. Instead, life becomes an exciting adventure because, with Christ in us and His Spirit guiding us, we never know what to expect. One thing we can be sure of, however, is that whatever happens to us in life, whatever transpires when we "show up," ultimately it will serve our good and the good of those we come in contact with. In the words of Paul, "And we know that all things work together for good to those who love God, to those who are the called according to His purpose" (Romans 8:28).

He can take your most humiliating defeat and turn it into a great victory.

Did you catch that? *All* things work together for good. Not *some* things or only positive and happy things but *all* things. Even the bad things. If you love God and are called according to His purpose (and every believer is), then God can and will use every circumstance and situation of your life for your good. He can take your most humiliating defeat and turn it into a great victory. He can transform your worst experiences into your richest learning and growing encounters. He can bring you from failure to success and from frustration to fulfillment.

If you are in a season right now where you are serving someone else's dream while yours is on hold, be patient; your season is coming. Ecclesiastes 3:1 says, "To everything there is a season, a time for every purpose under heaven." *Everything* has its season and *every* purpose has its time. If you are walking with the Lord and your dream is postponed, take comfort in the knowledge that He is in the process of preparing you for the day when you will walk in your destiny.

In the meantime, learn all you can where you are. Consider every day an opportunity to grow. Remember that nothing God ever does is wasted or without purpose. He has you where you are for a reason and if you ask Him, He will help you see your situation from His perspective: a perspective of hope and promise and prosperity and fruitfulness, a perspective of dreams realized and destiny fulfilled.

Remember from Chapter Six that the apostle Paul knew what it was like to pursue a dream. His dream was to

...gain Christ and be found in Him, not having my own righteousness, which is from

the law, but that which is through faith in Christ, the righteousness which is from God by faith; that I may know Him and the power of His resurrection, and the fellowship of His sufferings, being conformed to His death, if, by any means, I may attain to the resurrection from the dead (Philippians 3:8–11).

Paul likened his pursuit to a race with a great prize at the end:

Not that I have already attained, or am already perfected; but I press on, that I may lay hold of that for which Christ Jesus has also laid hold of me. Brethren, I do not count myself to have apprehended; but one thing I do, forgetting those things which are behind and reaching forward to those things which are ahead, I press toward the goal for the prize of the upward call of God in Christ Jesus (Philippians 3:12–14).

Wherever you are right now in your "race," don't despair; don't get discouraged; don't give up; and above all, don't sell out! Keep moving forward. Your "crossroads" is just ahead.

PERSONAL DREAM JOURNAL

CHAPTER TWELVE

Ain't Sellin' My Soul

Robert Johnson and who knows how many others went down to The Crossroads to make a deal with the devil. Or so the story goes. Is it true? No one knows for sure. But true or not, why anyone would want to sell his soul to the devil or make any other kind of deal with that loser is beyond me. Knowing what we know about the devil and his character, why would anyone want to have anything to do with him?

After all, the devil is really way overrated. Jesus totally defeated him, and as believers and followers of Jesus, we have no reason or cause to fear the devil.

Don't Take Your Dreams to the Grave

Jesus Himself said of the devil, "He was a murderer from the beginning, and does not stand in the truth, because there is no truth in him. When he speaks a lie, he speaks from his own resources, for he is a liar and the father of it" (John 8:44). Simon Peter said, "Be sober, be vigilant; because your adversary the devil walks about like a roaring lion, seeking whom he may devour. Resist him, steadfast in the faith, knowing that the same sufferings are experienced by your brotherhood in the world" (1 Peter 5:8–9). James, the brother of our Lord, wrote, "Submit yourselves therefore to God. Resist the devil, and he will flee from you" (James 4:7 KJV). A murderer, a liar, the father of lies, one who will flee when resisted; does this sound like someone we should be afraid of? Sure, Peter describes the devil as being "like a roaring lion," but a lion roars only when it has no prey. If the devil is a lion (and Peter only says he is like a lion), then he is a toothless lion.

Once the devil is revealed for the loser that he really is, we will look on him with amazement and be thoroughly under-whelmed. Jesus defeated the devil on our behalf, and we can now walk with Him in triumphant victory. Satan is a defeated enemy whom we need not fear. In Christ we even have the power to put him to flight simply by standing up to him in the name of Jesus.

Watch Out for the Dream Stealer

The devil may be a defeated loser but that doesn't mean he cannot still cause trouble. Be on the alert for he'll steal your dream if you give him half a chance. Or more accurately, he will influence or deceive you into abandoning your dream out of discouragement or despair or into surrendering it for something less that may in itself be good, but nonetheless, not the best that you could have had.

Most of the time, the fight for our soul is really a battle for our dreams.

Most of the time, the fight for our soul is really a battle for our dreams. After all, it is our dreams, passions, and desires that fire our soul and drive us to become who we are. They help define our identity. The devil's desire is to deceive us into forfeiting our destiny for something of a lesser status; in other words, to give up a piece of who we are. That is why we must always be alert to his schemes and not allow ourselves to be taken in by his lies. He may be a toothless lion, but if we're not careful, his roar can still intimidate us into making rash or unwise decisions. He can feed our discouragement over the delay in our dream fulfillment to the point where we give up on it altogether and resign ourselves to being and doing less than we had dreamed.

More often than not our fight isn't even with the devil as much as it is with ourselves. Too often we allow good things to become the enemy of the best things in our lives. What I mean is that sometimes we are too ready to settle for something good rather than hold out for the best. None of us would willingly or knowingly surrender our dreams for something that we knew was evil, wrong, or bad for us. But we might be tempted to compromise for something good, even if it's less than what we really want, especially if we fear that nothing better will come along.

Suppose you have been holding out for your dream for a long time. You have been waiting patiently and hopefully, looking forward to the time when you can do what you've always dreamed of doing. Time is passing, however, and you're getting worried that unless you act soon it will be too late. Suddenly an opportunity comes your way that sounds pretty good, even though it's not everything you want. Because you're anxious and desperate you think, "I'd better grab this while it's here. I may not get another chance like this. I should strike while the iron is hot." You go for it and you achieve it and it brings you a moderate degree of success and satisfaction. But deep inside you still wonder if you made the right decision. Something gnaws at your insides that you may have passed up your dream for something less; that you may have sacrificed the best in favor of the good.

Don't sell out! Don't sell your soul! Don't settle for the good when you can have the best! Don't give in to thoughts of compromise. Go to the Lord and ask Him to confirm your dream. Ask Him to reveal whether this opportunity is a stepping stone to your dream or merely a false path that will take you farther from it. Remember that He who planted the dream in your heart can and will bring it to fulfillment in your life if you allow Him to do it in His time and in His way. Don't settle for the good just because you think you may not get anything better. No matter where you are right now, no matter what your dream is, and no matter how far away your dream seems to be, God can bring it to complete fulfillment—instantly—when the time is right. Just remember that His timing may not be the same as yours.

Don't Allow Others to Steal Your Dream

Watch out also to make sure you do not allow other people to steal your dream. I don't mean people you may be serving right now to help them realize their dreams; that may be your training ground. I mean watch out for people who don't know about your dream or who don't believe in your dream who could steal it by discouraging you. It could be a family member or a friend, a work colleague or a boss; it could be anybody.

Nobody understands your vision or your dream better than you do. Be careful who you share your dream with. If you share it with just anybody you set yourself up for comments like, "Why would you want to do that?" or "You don't have the right skills," or "What makes you think you have what it takes?" or "It'll never work"...you get the idea. That's why it is so important to find and confide in people who believe in you, people who will support and encourage you. They don't even necessarily have to believe in your dream (although it helps) as long as they believe in *you*. As long as they believe in you they can help you believe in yourself, and when you believe in yourself, half the battle is already won.

Nobody understands your vision or your dream better than you do.

The Bible gives a powerful illustration of the tragic consequences of a stolen dream. The story is found in Numbers 13:1–14, 25. Moses had led the Israelites out of Egypt and into the Sinai wilderness. God had delivered them from their Egyptian pursuers by parting the Red Sea so they could cross over on dry land. He had fed them and provided water for them in the desert and had brought them to the very edge of the Promised Land. All they had to do was cross the river and possess the land as God had promised. This was their dream. This was what they had looked forward to ever since leaving Egypt.

Before entering the land, however, Moses sent 12 spies, one from each tribe, to bring back word regarding the fruitfulness of the land and the nature and disposition of the people who lived there. After 40 days the spies returned with a huge cluster of grapes and gave their report. The land was fertile and fruitful and very desirable, but the people who lived there were strong and had fortified cities. Ten of the spies said that taking the land was impossible. Only Joshua and Caleb kept faith that God would bring the Israelites victory.

Unfortunately, the children of Israel allowed the bad report of ten of the spies to steal their dream. Part of their problem was that they didn't really believe that

Don't Take Your Dreams to the Grave

God could do what He had promised, despite all the wonders He had already performed on their behalf. They didn't trust in His ability to give them victory over the strong people who lived in the land.

In the end, the people rebelled against Moses and Aaron (and therefore against God also) and refused to enter the land. They gave up their dream in exchange for the hope of returning to Egypt, which in retrospect looked better to them than their current circumstances. But they never made it back to Egypt. Because of their rebellion, God consigned them to wander in the wilderness of Sinai for 40 years until every member of that rebellious generation died. Of that generation, only Joshua and Caleb, who had kept the faith, lived to see the dream of the Promised Land fulfilled.

A stolen or surrendered dream can be costly! Don't let it happen to you!

A stolen or surrendered dream can be costly! Don't let it happen to you! Fix your vision squarely on the best that God has for you. Follow Him and when He reveals to you that your season has come, go for it like killing snakes on a hot day!

Let Your Gift Make Room for You

As I mentioned in Chapter Three, when I took the leap to follow my dream, I left behind a secure and fruitful ministry as associate pastor in one of the fastest growing churches in America. Those were great years. I had a great salary with great benefits. I worked with great people—thousands of people whom I loved and who loved me and appreciated my ministry. For a long time I felt like I was in Heaven. At the time Sherri and I went to that church it was the right time for them and we were the right people for the job.

I said all that to stress the fact that even though I was not pursuing *my* dream at that time, that does not mean that I was not in the right place doing the right thing. I was. At that time in my life, that's where I needed to be. Although I was serving someone else's dream, I was also in a time of preparation for fulfilling my own. I just didn't know it then.

Over the years I have learned that the absence of peace in my life is one way that God uses to move me from my place of comfort into His place of peace. Not until the day I first began feeling dissatisfied did I suspect that something was amiss. Somehow I began to sense inside that our time at this church was ending. Nothing was wrong at the church; I just had a gut feeling that it was time for a change. Although I wouldn't have described it this way then, looking back, I can say now that my season of serving someone else's dream was coming to an end and the season for fulfilling my own dream was dawning. The time of my preparation was coming to a close and God was preparing to launch me in a new direction.

I don't know when I first recognized the dream that suddenly grew up in my heart again. At the time, I wasn't even sure exactly what the dream was. All I knew was that it was there. I think that part of my problem was that I was afraid to talk about my dream. It may be that I was simply too scared to let myself really believe that it was possible, that after all these years my dream might actually start coming to pass.

Some of this I was not consciously aware of. As I mentioned in Chapter Three, for a long time I thought (or assumed) that my discontent meant that I was supposed to pastor my own church. My point is that even as my sense of unrest grew, my awareness of the dream in me grew as well, but my understanding of the nature of my dream and how it could or would be fulfilled evolved over time.

This period of time during which I knew the dream was in me and that I was settling for something else was filled with some of the most difficult days I had experienced in years. I had to face up to the possibility that the position I was in could be the last thing I did with my life. Please understand me when I say again that there was nothing wrong with that position. I know many great men and women of God who serve other people's visions all their lives, and that is a wonderful calling. For awhile, it was the calling for Sherri and me. But not anymore.

I kept asking myself the question, "Can you be happy doing this for the rest of your life and not pursuing your dreams?" Could I see myself being happy or at peace doing what I was doing and never touching those gifts and the calling that God had placed in my heart? I wrestled with that question for months. It wasn't until that February day in 2000, when somewhere on I-55 between Jackson and Memphis Sherri and I took the leap into our future, that I finally understood what I was supposed to do. It wasn't until I dropped my safety net and stepped out of my comfort zone that the peace of God fully came over me and confirmed that I had made the right decision. It was scary and exhilarating all at once. I hadn't sold my soul to the good. I was preparing to go for the best.

143

Don't Take Your Dreams to the Grave

Sometimes compromise is necessary, but other times it is the worst thing you can do. It all depends on who is asking: God or man. As I said in Chapter Five, there are seasons when you must serve someone else's vision. But if you are faithful, the time will come when you will receive that which is your own. The season will arrive when your gift makes room for you: "A man's gift makes room for him, and brings him before great men" (Proverbs 18:16). If you are still in waiting mode, don't press the issue. Don't make the mistake of moving ahead of God. Think of it this way: God has gone ahead of you to prepare the way so that when you arrive the stage will already be set, and everything will be in place. Let your gift make room for you and the Lord will elevate you when your season comes.

God desires that we learn to walk in faith, taking each step as He reveals it and trusting Him for the full journey.

Step by Step

That day on I-55 Sherri and I took the first step toward the dream. As soon as we did, the rest of

144

God's plan for our lives started to unfold. Notice that I said the first step. The will of God is a process of discovery. Step by step, piece by piece, God unfolds His will to us. More often than not, He reveals to us at any given moment only what we need to take the next step. Only in rare instances will He open up the full picture for us to see at once. That can be scary for those of us who prefer to know everything up front before we start. But God desires that we learn to walk in faith, taking each step as He reveals it and trusting Him for the full journey.

I like what Paul says in Ephesians 2:10, particularly as rendered in *The Amplified Bible*:

> *For we are God's [own] handiwork (His workmanship), recreated in Christ Jesus, [born anew] that we may do those good works which God predestined (planned beforehand) for us (taking paths which He prepared ahead of time), that we should walk in them—living the good life which He prearranged and made ready for us to live* (Ephesians 2:10 AMP).

I was in a business meeting once where we were attempting to make some decisions but nothing was getting done. Finally one of the men stood up and said, "The steps of a good man are ordered by the Lord (Psalm 37:23), but in order for his steps to be ordered he has to be taking them." The key to walking in the will of God is to go step by step as He lights your path.

Sometimes you may have no clear sense of what God wants you to do next. In that situation, the best thing to do is to keep doing the last thing you know God told you to do. When He has something else for you to do, He will let you know. Whatever you do, *don't stop*. Faith is never static; it is always moving. That's why the Bible calls faith a "walk." The important thing is to walk *with* God, not ahead of Him. He already knows the way He has set for you and everything it will take to get you there.

I said that God shows us only one step at a time because He wants us to learn to trust Him as we walk with Him. There is, I believe, another reason also, and it has to do with His loving care for us. First Corinthians 2:9 says, "But as it is written: 'Eye has not seen, nor ear heard, nor have entered into the heart of man the things which God has prepared for those who love Him.'" God has dreams and plans for us that are greater than we can possibly imagine and if He showed the full picture to us all at once, the magnitude of His dream for us would so overwhelm us that we would be too scared even to start. We would look at it and say, "I can't possibly do that!" Not all at once. But step by step we can.

How do you walk into your dream? One step at a time. Each step will take you a little higher and a little farther and prepare you for the next step. Eventually you will reach the top, look behind you, and be utterly amazed at where God has brought you and what He has done in and through you.

The key is to keep moving toward the goal. Don't stop, don't compromise, don't quit, don't surrender, and above all, don't sell out. Don't settle for anything less than God's best for your life. No matter how big you think your dream is, God's dream for you is even bigger. Don't miss it by selling out early or stopping short of the goal. Walking into your dream is a process of one step after another and each step brings you that much closer. So get busy walking and watch your dream come to pass!

PERSONAL DREAM JOURNAL

CHAPTER THIRTEEN

Get Out the Boat

One day when I was at home working in my office my friend and bassist Jeff Wollenberg called. I was right in the middle of writing a song for my second CD, *Something Better*. Jeff had a distinctive, unmistakable way of talking on the phone. Whenever I answered one of his calls he would say, "Jimmie B!" He and I would talk several times a day. That day he asked, "What are you doing? Are you writing a song?"

I told Jeff that my song was based on the story in Matthew 14 about Peter walking on the water. "It's titled 'Get Out of the Boat,'" I told Jeff.

"No, no!" Jeff replied. "It's got to be 'Get Out the Boat'!" And that was it. The soul of the song was found in the title. To date, "Get Out the Boat" has been one of my most popular songs.

Safe in the Boat? Or Out in the Waves?

I have heard this story from Matthew 14 preached many times. Usually the focus is on Peter's lack of faith, which Jesus mentions. But sometimes I wonder why Peter was the focus of rebuke when there were 11 others who just sat in the boat where it was safe! Let's take a closer look at this story, which is found in Matthew 14:22–33.

Jesus had just performed the miracle of feeding 5,000 people with five loaves of bread and two fish. Now, while He dismissed the crowd, Jesus sent His disciples ahead of Him in the boat. Then He went off by Himself to pray. The disciples were crossing the Sea of Galilee, which is infamous for violent storms that blow up suddenly with little warning. Didn't Jesus know what was going to happen? Wasn't He aware of the approaching storm?

I believe He was. I believe Jesus knew all the time what was happening and what He was going to do. None of this was an accident. Jesus took advantage of many opportunities to teach His disciples about faith and to show them who He was. This was another of those times.

Sometime during the fourth watch of the night Jesus came to them, walking on the water. The fourth watch was from 3–6 a.m., so this was the middle of the night. For the men in this boat, even the seasoned fishermen like Peter, Andrew, James, and John, a storm on this lake was no laughing matter. They probably all had friends or acquaintances who had drowned in just such a storm. The fact that it was the middle of the night made it even worse. Because the "wind was contrary" they couldn't make any headway; they could neither proceed nor turn back. Let's face it: they were stuck. Now, all of a sudden, through the wind and the waves and the violent rocking of the boat, they see a mysterious figure walking toward them *across* the water! No wonder they thought it was a ghost!

Hearing their cries of fear, Jesus tried to set their minds at ease by saying, "Don't be afraid; it's Me." He even said, "Be of good cheer." In a storm-tossed boat in the middle of the night? From Jesus' perspective there was no problem. With the disciples it was another story. They needed to learn how to see their situation through Jesus' eyes. That's part of what this "teachable moment" was all about.

Understanding the frightening, even apparently life-threatening situation the disciples were in casts new light on Peter's actions. In the midst of all this turmoil, the rough fisherman said to Jesus, "If it's really You, tell me to walk to You on the water." Jesus immediately said, "Come on."

Would you have gotten out of the boat? Or would you have stayed with the others where it was "safe" (relatively speaking)? Despite its violent rocking, why leave the security of a perfectly good boat for the uncertainty of the waves? As my song asks, "Which one are you like: Peter or the brothers?" As far as I'm concerned, Peter showed a lot of faith.

Playing It Safe

Of course, everything went fine at first. Peter got "out the boat" and actually was walking toward Jesus on the water! It was working! Unfortunately, it didn't last. The moment Peter took his eyes off of Jesus and started paying attention to the strong wind and the waves whipping around him, he began to sink. That's always the way it is with faith. As long as we focus on Jesus we're fine. It's when we turn our thoughts and concerns to the things of the world that we get into trouble.

When Peter began to sink, he did the right thing: he called out to the Lord. Jesus reached out, took him by the hand, and said, "O you of little faith, why did you doubt?" As soon as Jesus and Peter stepped into the boat, the wind ceased. The sea was calm again. That's when the light bulb came on in the disciples' heads. They worshiped Jesus and said, "You really *are* the Son of God!"

So often when this story is told, the emphasis is placed on the smallness of Peter's faith. I think this misses the point. Think about it. Even if only for a few seconds, Peter did something he had never done before and which all his natural instincts as a sailor would have warned him against: he walked on water in the middle of a storm! Even when he began to sink and Jesus took his hand, the *two* of them still walked on the water back to the boat! Yet we usually speak of Peter's actions as a failure. I don't think so. Peter had enough faith to take a risk, get out of the boat, and walk to Jesus. He was willing to step out of the "safe" place and put himself completely in the hands of his Master, and his faith was not misplaced. After this event, Peter undoubtedly never thought of Jesus or himself in quite the same way again.

Jesus spoke to Peter about his faith but said nothing to the other disciples, possibly because they had not even made the attempt. They were playing it safe. "What? Me get out of this boat? Are you crazy? It may be rocking, but at least it's holding me up!"

Don't Take Your Dreams to the Grave

There's certainly something to be said for being in a safe place. We all want and need a sense of security. But sometimes the "safe" place can turn out to be the most dangerous place you can be, especially when God is trying to draw you out of your comfort zone into the true security of His will. The place of safety can become a trap preventing you from fulfilling the will of God for your life. It can prevent you from ever realizing your dream. More dreams have been lost for fear of trying than for probably any other reason. I know that for me there came a day when I had to say goodbye to the boat and get out on the water and start walking. Otherwise my dream would have remained only a dream.

The place of safety can become a trap preventing you from fulfilling the will of God for your life.

Nobody can fulfill his or her dream and stay in the "safe" place at the same time. At some point, you've got to get out of the boat. If you can see your dream, it can and will come to pass. In Jesus you have unlimited resources available. As long as you don't quit, you cannot fail.

What's worse than failure? Never even trying in the first place. That was the problem of the other

11 disciples in the boat. They opted for safety and achieved nothing. Peter chose the risk and grew from the experience. His effort may not have been a complete success, but neither was it a failure. The important thing is that he tried.

Redneck Disciple

Peter was the right kind of guy for this job. Impulsive, rough-edged, hot-tempered, Peter was prone at times to put his mouth in motion before his brain was in gear. In a manner of speaking, you could say that Peter was the "redneck" of the disciples. He was ready to fight at the drop of a sword. But here's the real proof: John 21:2–5 says that Peter and some of the other disciples spent all night fishing but caught nothing. Only a redneck will fish all night long! But that's not all. Verse 7 also says (in King James and a few other versions) that Peter was fishing naked. Now that's *really* redneck! Some other versions translate it as Peter having removed his outer garment, so he may have been fishing in his underwear. Either way, naked or in his underwear, Peter was the redneck of the group.

Peter was always the first to jump in where others feared to tread. He tried walking on water and it almost worked. In John 21, he gets his feet wet again. What's his motivation? Jesus is standing on the shore (this is after His resurrection) and has just told them where to cast their nets for a huge catch of fish after they have tried all night without success. Impetuous, redneck Peter, in his eagerness to get to Jesus, pulls on his clothes and jumps overboard. Not bothering to try walking on water this time, he swims to shore leaving the others to haul in the catch and bring the boat in by themselves.

This was the guy who had denied Jesus three times only hours after pledging unwavering loyalty to Him. Now this lakeside encounter would be Peter's restoration and a defining moment in his life. Three times, once for each denial, Jesus asks Peter, "Do you love Me?" When Peter says, "Yes," Jesus responds, "Feed My sheep." For the rest of his life Peter did just that. Peter may have been a redneck, but he loved Jesus and he knew Jesus loved him. Peter may have been a redneck, but he was never afraid to get out of the boat, to step outside the status quo, and take some risks for Jesus.

Pursuing Your Dream Involves Taking Risks

Risk taking is one side of the faith life that we don't hear much preaching or teaching about. A risk is a hazard, danger, or peril. To take a risk means exposing ourselves to possible loss, injury, or destruction. Certainly our natural bent, and most often the course of common sense, is to do our best to stay as far away from those things as possible. Risk is inherent in the Christian life because that life is a faith walk and faith involves risk.

Those crossroads where a decision lies before us are what we can also call *kairos* moments from the Lord. *Kairos* is a Greek word that means "opportune time." A *kairos* moment is an opportune moment that is of strategic importance because it does not come by very often. It's the Lord's way of saying, "Here's your chance. What are you going to do with it?" So whenever the Lord brings a *kairos* moment our way we have to be prepared to take a step of faith. In other words, we have to be ready to "Get Out the Boat" and go for it. The only other choice is to sit tight and risk missing the opportunity. Personally, I'd rather risk the adventure of the open waves than sit safely in the boat and risk passing up the chance of a lifetime.

Risk takers are a rare breed of people, especially those who can wait for the voice of God before acting rather than risking just for risk's sake. Whether we like it or not, taking risks is a part of life and a huge part of the faith life. I love hanging out with risk takers who aren't "flakes," if you know what I mean. My kind of risk takers are interesting, adventuresome, and sometimes radical people who are in love with life and with the Lord; people who are in touch with their "wild side" but never allow themselves to go off the deep end.

Walk in Faith, Not Anxiety

When Sherri and I left our positions at the church in March 2000 we were taking a risk. Sure, we were obeying God but it was still risky. We had no idea exactly what was going to happen or what direction our lives would take. So for a little while we were a couple of pretty anxious people. After all, we were stepping out of the boat and weren't absolutely certain whether or not the water would hold us up. Once we did, however, and found ourselves walking those waves, there was no turning back. You'll never know if you can walk on water and achieve your dream until you commit to "Get Out the Boat" and try it. That's why the people who never try and who never risk anything will never achieve their dream or fulfill their destiny.

A certain amount of anxiety is normal when you first start aggressively pursuing your dream because you rarely have all the details worked out ahead of time. If you are following the Lord, however, you shouldn't *live* in anxiety. Anxiety is first cousin to fear and both are enemies of faith. That's why Paul's counsel in Philippians is so important:

> *Be anxious for nothing, but in everything by prayer and supplication, with thanksgiving, let your requests be made known to God; and the peace of God, which surpasses all understanding, will guard your hearts and minds through Christ Jesus* (Philippians 4:6–7).

Whenever you are going after your dream there will always be some unknowns and uncertainties, and these can generate a certain amount of anxiety. But if you are following the Lord—if He has brought you to a *kairos* moment and shown you that your season has come—in the midst of those unknowns He will give you His peace that you are doing the right thing. Eventually, His peace will supplant the anxiety you feel.

Make no mistake about it: pursuing your dream means taking risks, even when you're following the Lord. For one thing, you run the risk of family and friends not understanding you. They may not comprehend what you are trying to do. After all, it's your dream, not theirs. Once your course is charted and your intention is set, don't let anyone discourage you or dissuade you.

Don't Take Your Dreams to the Grave

You may also risk your reputation if people who know you think your dream is impractical or unrealistic. They may think you've gone crazy. Let them think what they want. Don't squelch your dream or take it to the grave for the sake of someone else's opinion.

Depending on the nature of your dream, another risk you run when pursuing it is the risk of losing the "safety net" of a secure job, steady paycheck, and good benefits you have become accustomed to. In truth, the only real safety net is to walk in the center of God's will for your life. God has committed Himself and placed His reputation on the line in His promise to care and provide for and bless and prosper all those who will trust Him and follow His way. Proverbs 10:3a says, "The Lord will not allow the righteous soul to famish." Isaiah 41:10 records this promise from God: "Fear not, for I am with you; be not dismayed, for I am your God. I will strengthen you, yes, I will help you, I will uphold you with My righteous right hand."

Yes, there are risks in pursuing your dream, just as there are in any worthwhile undertaking. But when God has brought you into your season you can proceed anxiety-free in the confidence and knowledge that if you walk in faith and stand firm, keeping your vision before you, it will come to pass. You *will* succeed and you *will* walk in your dream.

Abram Had to "Get Out the Boat"

As I said before, God's dream for us is bigger than we can imagine and certainly bigger than our dream for ourselves. Abram from the Old Testament is a good example. Here's a man with a beautiful wife named Sarai who unfortunately is barren; she cannot have children. What was Abram's dream for himself? A son. All Abram wanted all his life was a son to carry on his name and family line, but it seemed as though that was not going to happen. One day when Abram and Sarai were both beyond child-bearing age the Lord came to Abram:

Now the Lord had said to Abram: "Get out of your country, from your family and from your father's house, to a land that I will show you. I will make you a great nation; I will bless you and make your name great; and you shall be a blessing. I will bless those who bless you, and I will curse him who curses you; and in you all the families of the earth shall be blessed (Genesis 12:1–3).

Don't Take Your Dreams to the Grave

Abram's dream was to have a son. God's dream was to give Abram a son—and much more. God's dream was to raise up through that son an entire nation of descendants for Abram — a nation through which all the people of the earth would be blessed. Abram's dream for himself involved a son; God's dream for Abram involved the world.

God's promise to Abram hinged on Abram first getting out of the boat. Before he could become the father of a great nation he had to leave his own father's house. Before his name could be made great he had to start walking. Before he could become a blessing he had to "Get Out the Boat."

The risk in faith comes in trusting God with everything we are and have...

Abram took a risk when he left home but he never looked back because he had a God-given vision before him. That vision sustained him through the long journey from his home in what is present-day Iraq to his new home in what is present-day Israel. It sustained him through the 25 years he had to wait from the time God's promise of a son was given to the time when the promise was fulfilled. In fact, Abram's vision carried him through the rest of his life.

Faith always carries risk. We might not like it, but it's true. Hebrews 10:38 says that the just will live by faith while Hebrews 11:6 says that without faith it is impossible to please God. In other words, we must have faith in order to be right with God. The risk in faith comes in trusting God with everything we are and have; being willing to place our comfort, our name, our stability, and our very survival on His Word and step out of the boat.

When Sherri and I were facing the water as the only stable place for us to be, I found that I had to work a lot on my patience. I learned that for a vocational minister, the phrase "living by faith" was code language that meant "no salary." We risked everything we had to obey God and follow the dream even when we were still uncertain what form that dream would take. Like Abram, we didn't know exactly where we were going. God had said, "Go," and we were going. That's all that mattered.

The more we went the more I discovered that the dream in my heart was far bigger than I could admit at first. God took us into it in stages; otherwise the magnitude of what we were doing would have blown us away. Once we got out of the boat—once we stepped out on faith—the Lord took over and walked us step by step into our dream. He is the dream giver and the dream fulfiller, but you've got to be willing to "Get Out the Boat."

How about you? Are you ready to "Get Out the Boat" and start doing some water walking? That's where your dream is: in the water with Jesus. Don't sit in the boat tightly gripping the gunwales. Take the risk. Get in touch with your wild side. Stand up, step over the side, and walk the waves to Jesus. Keep your eyes on Him and He will carry you all the way to the finish.

CHAPTER FOURTEEN

The Dream of Finishing

Throughout this book I have been talking about the importance of dreams; the importance of keeping your dreams alive in your heart; the importance of pursuing your dreams; the importance of reaching for your full potential and not taking your dreams to the grave. Nothing is sadder than a person of potential to die unfulfilled. It is impossible to calculate the loss to the church and to the world of the contributions of people whose dreams were squelched, snuffed out, lost, or destroyed because of discouragement, disillusionment, distraction, disappointment, disbelief, or even premature death.

In a poem called "The Voiceless," 19th-century American poet Oliver Wendell Holmes wrote:

Don't Take Your Dreams to the Grave

We count the broken lyres that rest

Where the sweet wailing singers slumber,—

But o'er their silent sister's breast

The wild flowers who will stoop to number?

A few can touch the magic string,

And noisy Fame is proud to win them,—

Alas for those that never sing,

But die with all their music in them!

I don't intend to die with any of my music left in me, either literally or figuratively; I intend to die empty! I hope you do, too. That's what this book is all about.

God has given you a dream—a destiny that only you can fulfill. Maybe you're having a hard time identifying your dream because it has been suppressed or hidden for so long. Rest assured; it's still there. God gave you a dream and His gifts and calling are irrevocable (see Romans 11:29). Ask God to resurrect your dream in your heart. Get in touch with the "wild man" inside and grab hold of your dream once more. God doesn't do anything by accident or without purpose. What God planted *in* you He wants to fulfill in and *through* you. Otherwise, He wouldn't have given it to you.

166

Everybody has a dream. Everybody needs a dream. I hope your life is full of dreams: for life, marriage, children, profession; the chance to make a significant contribution to others' lives. Whatever your dreams, don't let them die and don't let anybody steal them. Dreams make our lives rich, exciting, challenging, meaningful, and purposeful. Dreams make our lives worth living.

Whatever your dreams, don't let them die and don't let anybody steal them.

I love hanging out with people who have dreams and have seen them come true. Their joy and enthusiasm for life are infectious. You'll never meet happier, healthier, more satisfied, more fulfilled, or more inspiring people than those who are living their dream.

Hope is a form of dreaming. I'm not talking about the kind of "hope" that says, "I hope it doesn't rain today" or "I hope I get that raise" or whatever. I'm talking about the kind of hope that gives people the strength to hold out and carry on because they know a better day is coming. I'm talking about the kind of hope that finds its source in the love and the promises of God. Hope is essential to life. People can endure the loss of almost anything except hope. Once hope is gone, death is not far behind.

There is one particular dream that I hope you have in your heart, for without it none of your other dreams will matter. I hope you have a *dream of finishing.* Unless you have a dream of finishing you probably will never fulfill any of your dreams.

At 22, right after I was saved, I analyzed my life and realized that I had never finished anything. Sure, I was still young, but it still shocked me. What a waste! And if that's a waste, think how much worse it would be to reach the end of a long life of 70 or 80 years or more and come to the same conclusion!

I looked at my failure to finish anything as it pertained to my salvation and I said to the Lord, "Lord, if You will help me to do this for just a year, I believe that I will be able to do it for the rest of my life." It has now been 28 years since I uttered that prayer.

We must have a dream of finishing—a vision inside of us that will keep us looking beyond the chaos and confusion of the moment to the victory and fulfillment at the end and help us to stay focused on Jesus no matter what.

Bill Wilson is a man who started a nationally known children's ministry in New York City. One day he was attacked and shot in the face. In an article about his ordeal he was asked whether or not he was going to continue his work. He said, "The two hardest things in life are *starting* and *finishing*. And I'm going to finish."

I'm going to finish, too. What about you? I hope you have that kind of resolve in your heart, that you are going to finish no matter what.

Finishing Is a New Testament Theme

Jesus had a dream of finishing. The night before He was crucified, Jesus prayed to His Father:

> *I have glorified You on the earth.* ***I have finished the work*** *which You have given Me to do. And now, O Father, glorify Me together with Yourself, with the glory which I had with You before the world was* (John 17:4–5 emphasis added).

From the very beginning of His ministry Jesus had a dream of finishing. He knew where He was headed and was determined that nothing would deter Him from fulfilling His Father's will. Jesus' dream was to carry out perfectly everything His Father gave Him to do. His dream of finishing was on His mind even as He hung on the cross. According to

John 19:30, Jesus' last words before dying were, "It is finished!" In other words, "I have completed My mission"; "I have fulfilled My purpose"; "I have done what I came to do"; "I have fulfilled My dream"; "I am dying *empty!*" I can easily imagine that there was a tone of exultation and deep satisfaction in Jesus' voice as He spoke those words.

> *"I have fulfilled My purpose"; "I have done what I came to do"; "I have fulfilled My dream"; "I am dying empty!"*

The apostle Paul had a dream of finishing. He told the Philippians:

Brethren, I do not count myself to have apprehended; but one thing I do, forgetting those things which are behind and reaching forward to those things which are ahead, I press toward the goal for the prize of the upward call of God in Christ Jesus (Philippians 3:13–14).

To the Corinthians he said:

Do you not know that those who run in a race all run, but one receives the prize? Run in such a way that you may obtain it. And everyone who competes for the prize is temperate in all things. Now they do it to obtain a perishable crown, but we for an imperishable crown. Therefore I run thus: not with uncertainty. Thus I fight: not as one who beats the air. But I discipline my body and bring it into subjection, lest, when I have preached to others, I myself should become disqualified (1 Corinthians 9:24–27).

Toward the end of his life, Paul wrote to Timothy, his protégé and son in the faith:

For I am already being poured out as a drink offering, and the time of my departure is at hand. I have fought the good fight, I have finished the race, I have kept the faith. Finally, there is laid up for me the crown of righteousness, which the Lord, the righteous Judge, will give to me on that Day, and not to me only but also to all who have loved His appearing (2 Timothy 4:6–8).

Finishing the race is a theme that runs throughout the New Testament. Pointing to Jesus as our example, the Book of Hebrews encourages us to make a good finish:

Therefore we also, since we are surrounded by so great a cloud of witnesses, let us lay aside every weight, and the sin which so easily ensnares us, and let us run with endurance the race that is set before us, looking unto Jesus, the author and finisher of our faith, who for the joy that was set before Him endured the cross, despising the shame, and has sat down at the right hand of the throne of God (Hebrews 12:1–2).

What Does It Take to Finish?

We are supposed to finish. The Bible encourages us to finish. God wants us to finish. Jesus died for us so we could finish. But what does it take to finish?

1. We must determine that we are going to finish from the start.

We have to decide right off the bat that we are going to stick with this and finish it. It's the nature of God to finish. Isaiah 46:10 says of God, "Declaring the end from the beginning...." God declares the end from the beginning. We need some declarations in our lives: "Jesus, I'm going to stick with You no matter what. I'm going to walk with You no matter what. Even if I fail I am going to get up and head for the finish line." We need to declare our end from our beginning. It is God's nature to finish. We are created in the image and likeness of God, so it should also be our nature to finish.

2. Never quit.

This may sound simplistic, but if you don't have a quitter's vocabulary, you won't find the luxury of quitting. Again, it is part of God's nature not to quit. God finishes what He starts. Psalm 86:15 in *The Message* reads like this: "But you, O God, are both tender and kind, not easily angered, immense in love, and you never, never quit."

God never quits on us. Aren't you glad? Even when we have squandered our inheritance and sinned against God; even when we have corrupted this planet, God never quits on us. God will never use the word "quit" in speaking about us. It is not in His vocabulary. As children of God we should take on His nature and eliminate it from ours.

3. We must have help.

We cannot do it alone. Jesus knew that, which is why He said to His disciples:

Nevertheless I tell you the truth. It is to your advantage that I go away; for if I do not go away, the Helper will not come to you; but if I depart, I will send Him to you....However, when He, the Spirit of truth, has come, He will guide you into all truth; for He will not speak on His own authority, but whatever He hears He will speak; and He will tell you things to come. He will glorify Me, for He will take of what is Mine and declare it to you (John 16:7, 13–14).

Jesus promised to send the Holy Spirit to help us. I don't know about you, but I require a steady dose of help in my life. None of us can make a good finish on our own. We must have the help of the Holy Spirit. That's why Jesus sent Him to dwell in our hearts. As we walk with the Lord the Spirit will guide us into all truth and help us remember and understand the things Jesus taught. It is only with the help of the Holy Spirit that we have any real chance of realizing our dreams and fulfilling our destiny.

We also need the help of the local church. When Sherri and I got saved, we knew one thing: that we didn't know anything. I've met people who had been saved for three months and all of a sudden they're instant theologians; you can't teach them a thing. Sherri and

I weren't like that. We knew we needed the help of the local church so we became church people.

Don't try to go it alone. Jesus Christ established His church as a community—a group of believers united by a common faith who need each other to grow and learn and do the will of God together. No individual Christian can function properly alone and the church cannot function properly unless every member—every part of the body—is in place and working. If we have a dream of finishing, we need the help of the local church.

In addition, we all need the help of each other. There are some things we cannot conquer alone. Consider King David in the Old Testament: shepherd, warrior, musician, psalmist, giant-killer, lover of God; a man of many talents and capabilities. One day, however, David found himself with a giant in his life that he could not kill by himself:

> *When the Philistines were at war again with Israel, David and his servants with him went down and fought against the Philistines; and David grew faint. Then Ishbi-Benob, who was one of the sons of the giant, the weight of whose bronze spear was three hundred shekels, who was bearing a new sword,*

thought he could kill David. But Abishai the son of Zeruiah came to his aid, and struck the Philistine and killed him. Then the men of David swore to him, saying, "You shall go out no more with us to battle, lest you quench the lamp of Israel" (2 Samuel 21:15–17).

David was worn out from battle and a Philistine giant named Ishbi-Benob though he could finish off the Israelite king. But Abishai, one of David's mighty warriors, told the king, "You sit this one out. I'll take care of him." And he did.

We're no different from David. All of us from time to time need the help of others. Paul said, "Bear one another's burdens, and so fulfill the law of Christ" (Galatians 6:2). If we try to go it alone we end up with two bad situations: we are not available to help others when they need it and they are not around to help us when we need it. The wisdom of Ecclesiastes is appropriate here:

Two are better than one, because they have a good reward for their labor. For if they fall, one will lift up his companion. But woe to him who is alone when he falls, for he has no one to help him up. Again, if two lie down together, they will keep warm; but how can one be warm alone? Though one may be overpowered by another, two can withstand him. And a threefold cord is not quickly broken (Ecclesiastes 4:9–12).

It was no different with Jesus. On His way to the cross, Jesus became so exhausted from the beating and other abuse He had suffered that He could no longer carry His own cross. The Romans drafted a man named Simon of Cyrene to bear Jesus' cross the rest of the way. Even Jesus needed help from others.

There are things in life that we cannot do without each other if we are going to finish.

There are things in life that we cannot do without each other if we are going to finish.

How can we help each other?

First of all, we can be friends with each other. Proverbs 17:17 says, "A friend loves at all times, and a brother is born for adversity." This verse says "at all times." That means pretty times and ugly times, brilliant times and stupid times. We must in our own lives perfect the art of friendship.

177

Second, we have to be a safe place for each other—a place where people can come when they fail, which we all do. We must be a place where people can come and know they will be accepted even in their failure. Why? Because that's what Jesus did. Jesus came to a planet filled exclusively with millions upon millions of failures and with His arms open and love in His heart said, "I'll take them all."

We have to be people who are trustworthy and not shocked by sin. There's some pretty awful sin out there, but we need to remember that under the right circumstances any of us are capable of the worst things imaginable. It is only by the grace of God that we are spared.

Part of being a safe place also is learning to accept people as they are, not as we want them to be. It is not our place or our right to burden anyone else with false standards of appearance or behavior that they must adopt before we will accept them. Jesus accepted people as they were and loved them anyway; we must do the same. We must offer solutions, not criticism. And we must be those who will disperse power.

A third way we can help each other is to be façade-free. This means we have to be who we are all the time and not try to make people think we are someone we're not. Don't be a hypocrite. Remember that in Greek theater a "hypocrite" was an actor who wore different masks in different scenes so that it was hard to distinguish the real person. Don't be a mask-wearer. Once we become Christians our masks need to come off and stay off. People need to feel safe and unthreatened around us and the only way that can happen is if we are transparent and not afraid to be ourselves or to let others see us as we really are.

Fourth, we can help each other by picking each other up when we fall. I mentioned in Chapter Seven a minister I befriended who had fallen into moral sin. In fact, he committed adultery. Even though he confessed his sin and had submitted to the authority over him for reconciliation and restoration, they ended up taking almost everything away from him. They even publicly humiliated him in front of his children. I made it my intention to be a friend to that man because he needed somebody to pick him up. Today he is reinstated in ministry and is the pastor of a great church.

I have a good friend who recently was revealed to be a homosexual. I know that disqualifies him from ministry, but it does not disqualify him from being my friend. You can discard people all you want, but I'd just as soon carry somebody who's wounded to the throne of God and lay him at the feet of Jesus and let Jesus touch his life. And I'd just as soon be there in his life despising his sin while shining a light that says, "There's another way." Always in love.

As Bill Wilson said, "The two hardest things in life are starting and finishing." Are you going to finish? I'm not asking if you're going to fall down—we all do that—but are you going to finish regardless of the mistakes you make, regardless of the failures you experience, regardless of whether everything goes your way or not? Are you going to finish with Jesus? Are you going to stay there? Are you still going to let Him have access to your heart?

God has planted a dream in your heart. Where is that dream? What are you doing with it right now? Are you walking in your dream? If not, are you moving toward it? Or are you still in "standby mode" waiting for your season to come? Are you stuck in the trap of religion with your dream stifled and suffocating? Wherever you find yourself, God can fulfill your dream in His time and in His way. Trust in the Lord with all your heart. Don't depend on your own knowledge or understanding. Acknowledge God in all your ways and He *will* direct your paths.

Your dream is too precious to waste. Don't abandon your dream. Don't surrender and don't sell out. Above all, don't take your dream to the grave! Commit your way to the Lord and let Him bring you into your season. Get out of the boat and walk in faith on the waves. You have potential that God wants you to release and a destiny He wants you to fulfill. Your season is coming. Be patient, be faithful, and stand firm. Walk with the Lord and one of these days He will walk you right into your dream!

About the Author

Jimmie Bratcher's dedication to Jesus all started when he and his then-divorced wife Sherri remarried. Right there at the ceremony, they gave their lives to Jesus. From that point the Bratchers dedicated themselves to serving the local church. Jimmie started out as a worship leader/music minister, then became an associate pastor. In 2000 Jimmie and Sherri founded Ransom Ministries, a non-profit ministry dedicated to helping local pastors to experience growth and success in evangelistic services.

Today Jimmie Bratcher is a well-known, Gospel-preaching, blues-playing musician. With 25 years of experience in the music industry,

Jimmie released his first album, *Honey in the Rock*, in 2001, followed by *Something Better* in 2003. He and his wife Sherri travel extensively in North America and the United Kingdom ministering and performing in both Christian and secular arenas.